ACT IN SPORT

ACT IN SPORT
Improve Performance through Mindfulness, Acceptance, and Commitment

James Hegarty &
Christoph Huelsmann

DARK RIVER

Published in 2020 by Dark River, an imprint of Bennion Kearny Limited.

Copyright © Dark River

James Hegarty and Christoph Huelsmann have asserted their rights under the Copyright Designs and Patents Act 1988 to be identified as the authors of this work

ISBN: 9781911121978

All Rights Reserved. No part of this publication may be reproduced, stored in a retrieval system, or transmitted in any form or by any means, electronic, mechanical, photocopying, recording or otherwise, without the prior permission of the publisher.

This book is sold subject to the condition that it shall not, by way of trade or otherwise, be lent, re-sold, hired out or otherwise circulated without the publisher's prior consent in any form of binding or cover other than that it which it is published and without a similar condition including this condition being imposed on the subsequent purchaser.

Dark River has endeavoured to provide trademark information about all the companies and products mentioned in this book by the appropriate use of capitals. However, Dark River cannot guarantee the accuracy of this information.

Disclaimer of liability. This book does not contain medical advice. The medical information and any advice or instructions - as per the exercises and elsewhere - is provided for general information and educational purposes only. Accordingly, the use, reliance, or implementation of any advice contained within this book is solely at the reader's risk.

Published by Dark River, an imprint of Bennion Kearny Limited.
6 Woodside, Churnet View Road, Oakamoor, ST10 3AE, UK

About the Authors

James Hegarty PhD, FNZCCP, is a clinical psychologist and neuropsychologist. He has worked with individuals, groups and organisations. His long-term interest in the psychology of sports performance has led to consultation work with athletes and the mentoring of other psychologists. He has trained psychologists and other professionals in ACT and mindfulness techniques since 2005. In 2007, in recognition of his contribution to the profession, he was awarded a Fellowship of the New Zealand College of Clinical Psychologists. He works in private practice in Dunedin, New Zealand.

Christoph Huelsmann is a clinical psychologist with over 20 years' experience working in mental health, rehabilitation, and sport psychology, including as a performance psychologist with High Performance Sport New Zealand. He has experience of working directly with athletes and sport teams as well as teaching, and is currently working in private practice in Wellington, New Zealand.

Table of Contents

Foreword: Workouts for Mental Performance — 17

Introduction — 21
    FEAR and the Mind - What usually doesn't work — 24
    Who this book is for — 33
    Meet Conradand Wayne — 34

Chapter 1: What Is ACT? — 37
    How the Mind Works — 37
    Relational Frame Theory — 38
    What is ACT? — 42
    What ACT isn't — 47
    What ACT Is — 48
    ACT and Other Psychological Approaches — 50
        Acceptance — 54
        Defusion — 55
        Values and Committed Action — 56
        Self As Context — 58
        Contact with the Present Moment — 62
        Mindfulness and ACT — 63
    Summary — 65

Chapter 2: The Three Pillars 67
- The Three Pillars in Action 73
- Identifying Your Barriers to Performance: Step 1 84
- Mindfulness 98
  - The Finger Exercise 101
  - Posture in mindfulness practice 106
- Further suggestions 112
- Summary 116
- Things to Practise 117

Chapter 3: Values 118
- What Are Values? 122
- Values and Goals 124
- Discovering Values 130
  - Exercise One – The Funeral 130
  - Exercise Two – The Tombstone Exercise 132
  - Exercise Three – Values Identification 134
- Living Your Values 140
  - Exercise Four – Living your values 142
- Values in Sport 147
  - The 80th Birthday Exercise 148
  - Exercise Five – Values in the context of sport 150
  - Exercise Six – the Bull's Eye 152
- A Plan of Action 155
- Summary 157

Chapter 4: Passengers (Monsters) on the Bus — 159
The Journey — 160
Monsters on the Bus — 165
- Exercise One – Avoid — 167
- Exercise Two - Argue — 169
- Exercise Three – Acknowledge/Accept — 172
- Exercise Four - Action — 174
- Some thoughts on Monsters on the Bus — 176
- Diary of Reactive Habits I — 178
- Example One — 182
- Diary of Reactive Habits II — 184
- Example Two — 186
- Diary of Reactive Habits III — 187

Sensory Perception — 191
Things to practise — 194
Summary — 195

Chapter 5: The Anxious Passenger — 197
Anxiety and the humanmind — 200
- A Study on the effects of Acceptance and Control — 207
- A study on 'Catastrophic Performance Decline' — 215

Developing Acceptance and Courage — 220
- Leaning in Exercise — 221

Conrad harnessing the Tiger Inside — 230
- Interpretation of arousal and performance — 232

A time for calmness 234
Mind fulness, Defusion, and Anxiety 236
   Brain Imaging 239
Two strategies Conrad woulduse 241
Building flexible attention 242
   Building the Attention Muscle 242
   Exercise 1 – The Leaf Exercise 243
Summary 246

Chapter 6: Motivation, Willingness, and Commitment 248
   Holding your breath 250
The willingness to suffer for what matters ... 252
   Accepting and Defusing discomfort.
   Holding your breath, the second time 254
Making Excuses 258
   Mini exercise: Independence Training 263
   Mini exercise: Thoughts are just thoughts
   as a habit 264
Uncoupling 262
Doing what needs to be done:
freedom from thought 266
   Acting as if – Getting a foot in the door 270
The Power of 'acting as if': Counter Clockwise ... 271
Values and Motivation 274
Are you prepared to do whatittakes? 276

Two sides of the coin	277
Two sides of a coin exercise	279
Reducing Passenger Opportunities	280
Focus on process, not out come	281
Summary	284

Chapter 7: Self – Esteem, Self – Concept and the Tyranny of 'ME' 287

The Downside of Self – Esteem: I can vers us I feel	288
Fear of failure	291
Lack of commitment and effort	292
Blaming others	292
Feeling like a fraud	293
TheW alk – Through Exercise – Part One	301
TheWalk-Through Exercise	304
Example	307
The Walk – Through Exercise – Part Two	310
Things to practise	314
Summary	314

Chapter 8: Managing Passengers Everywhere: Wrapping it up and Integrating your Skills 317

How to manage bus passengers: Core Skills in a Nutshell	319
Being Present and Aware	319

   Knowing your why, and Doing what matters   320
   Being open and accepting   320
   Defusion skills   321
Aches and Pains   322
   1. Open and aware   325
   2. Doing what matters   326
   3. Open and accepting   326
Dealing with other people   330
Working out your Values as a Team   331
   1. Open and aware   336
   2. Doing what matters   337
Integrating mental skill practice into your life   338
Summary   340

Chapter 9: Trouble shooting   343
   I don't want to accept feeling bad!   348
   I don't get mindfulness   349
   I can't do mindfulness   353
   I don't have time   354
   When I do mindfulness,
   I don't have any thoughts   355
   I can't do the values exercise   356
   All my values are high   357
   I made changes but after a week or
   so I fall back into the same old habits   357
   Conclusion   358

Appendix 1: A list of ACT Exercises   361
  ACT Exercises by Function   362
  Additional Exercises   366
      Carry your thoughts around   366
      'Milk, Milk, Milk....'   368
      'Acceptance'   371

References   373

Download

Download the accompanying workbook to complement your learning and development.

Just visit: **www.BennionKearny.com/ACT**

Foreword: Workouts for Mental Performance

Sport presents a paradox for psychologists. Physical strength and conditioning dominate published training advice, but muscles work at the whim of the head and the heart. Sport is every bit as much psychological as it is physical.

It is unlikely that this gap is intentional. While thoughts and feelings are omni-present, it is easier to describe, model, and coach an athlete at how to kick a ball or run a course. And like the proverbial fish that never notices its own wetness, that same omnipresence of thoughts and feelings can result in a blindness toward how we interact with our own inner experiences.

Past efforts to address the "sport mind" have focused on waiving away our internal world, or artificially forcing change. Thanks to advances in behavioural psychology, today we have more effective practices that you can incorporate into your own training. With concerted and consistent effort, these practices will establish honed skills that you can employ in pursuit of the best version of yourself. Importantly, these skills will never ask you to spend fruitless effort trying to explain away or fighting with your thoughts or feelings.

This short and clear book will walk you through the foundational elements and tried and true practices of Acceptance and Commitment Therapy or Training (it is "ACT" in either form, and is pronounced as the word "act"). It lays out common sport scenarios where you are likely to put these ACT skills into practice, creating an overall set known as "psychological flexibility".

ACT, like sport, is best learned in the doing. To provide you with the most effective tools and a hands on experience, the authors have integrated meaningful 'workouts' with each chapter. We know it is tempting to fly by these 'workouts' as you read from one cover to another. Don't. You bought this book for a reason. Something important to you has brought you here. Something may seem to be in the way. In the service of that important thing, are you willing to commit to engage with each of these 'workouts' to strengthen your own sport mind?

Working out your sport mind has a lot of similarities to working out your body. When you first start, you can expect discomfort or disorientation, and it will take you a while to get through the sets. But, just like your muscles, your sport mind will strengthen. As you continue with regular practice, you will be able to finish your sets sooner, be able to start ramping up the reps, and eventually be able to sustain your effort for bigger or longer challenges. Best of all, because our thoughts and feelings are always with us, there are no dumbbells or running shoes to tote around. If you want to get in a quick set, do it. Right where you are.

One difference between working out your sport mind and working out your body is, as your mind gets stronger, the lifts get lighter. This paradox mirrors one of the more common statements about ACT. "ACT doesn't help you feel better. It helps you feel better." By becoming better at connecting with your thoughts and feelings in a functional and complementary manner, you will spend less time playing tug-of-war with yourself. You will be more able to commit your strength to moving toward what matters to you in sport – and in life. And all of that while feeling everything that comes along with that deeply personal endeavour.

Congratulations on taking the first step toward what matters to you. This book will show you the next steps toward a stronger and more flexible you.

Patrick Smith
University of Nevada, USA Cycling Licensed Coach

Steven C. Hayes
Foundation Professor of Psychology, University of Nevada and originator and co-developer of Acceptance and Commitment Therapy

Introduction

The science behind functioning in high-pressure sporting situations has made some major advances over the last decades. Our understanding of the 'mind' and its processes now offers a number of good explanations and insights.

One of these advances is a methodology referred to as 'Acceptance and Commitment Therapy', or ACT.

The theory behind ACT can explain a lot of what might have happened to the players during the Soccer World Cup of 2014 when Brazil suffered one of the most crushing defeats in sporting history. In front of a disbelieving Estádio Mineirão crowd, the host nation was taken apart by Germany in a devastating 7-1 loss.

During this game, a few extraordinary things happened. For example, Germany scored four goals within six minutes, two of which were separated by just 69 seconds, the shortest timespan ever in any World Cup game. They won by the biggest margin in any World Cup final or semi-final, and Brazil suffered the biggest loss of any hosting nation in a World Cup.

How did this happen?

During the game, it became obvious to spectators and players alike that something peculiar was occurring, something that had little to do with the ordinary tension and mistakes that can happen during a high-level knockout game between two great soccer nations.

Indeed, later on, Germany's captain Phillip Lahm said that it got to a point were even he felt 'very uneasy' about what was unfolding and that, on some level, he did not enjoy the game. He said, 'No one wants the opponent to make mistakes that usually don't happen at this level' (Stern, 2014).

Player Toni Kroos attributed the countless mistakes of the Brazilian players to the somewhat extraordinary outside pressure they were facing. In the host country, nothing less than winning the World Cup would do! But then, this would have happened many times to other national teams previously, without such dire consequences.

In the weeks leading up to this game Brazil's coach, Felipe Scolari, complained that his players had been crying too much and called upon a sport psychologist after the knockout game against Chile (something we should, maybe, not mention here as it was not crowned with much success). Brazil won narrowly (in a penalty shootout) but, during the game, some players suffered something akin to an emotional meltdown.

The national media in Brazil later mocked the players for sobbing before the penalty shootout had even started! Captain Thiago Silva was so nervous that he could not participate in the shootout himself, and watched from the side-lines. In spite of this remarkable decision by the captain of the team, Silva expressed confidence that Brazil could perform again under pressure, albeit with the help of a psychologist who had taught them 'to relax'.

Anyway, back to the Germany game.

In the 11th minute of the semi-final, the German forward Thomas Mueller opened the scoring as a result of a huge defensive mistake by David Luiz. In the 24th minute, with the second goal, Brazil fell apart. They were not able to reassemble themselves, and mistake followed mistake; three more goals were conceded within the following six minutes, and the game was lost in almost record time.

The Guardian newspaper later described events as follows.

'The faces of the Brazilian players, psychologically groomed though they were, went through the gamut of emotions from shock to fear, and from fear to horrified despair. Under the German attack, they blundered about in a haze of mildness and lost 7-1.'

Of course, we can only assume what happened in the minds of these players. But we can make some informed guesses in light of the players' responses during the game and through ACT...

FEAR and the Mind –
What usually doesn't work

For a long time, the prevailing view in sport psychology and therapy had been that sport performance and life can be improved by overcoming and changing negative thoughts and feelings.

Acceptance and Commitment Therapy (ACT) is a more recent, and unique, behaviour change approach that addresses these issues by altering the very ground on which normal change strategies rest. Instead of focusing on the need to change unwanted thoughts and feelings, ACT emphasizes the role of how we relate to thoughts and feelings. Instead of changing them, one of its main ideas is that acceptance of unwanted inner experiences, and defusion from them, frees us up so that we can have a more vital life doing the things we need to do.

One example of using ACT would be when a person is having feelings of anxiety; strategies can then be used to let them run their course without making them worse (or letting them ruin performance). The 'how to' of this is something we are going to explain in this book.

The how to – of how we relate to thoughts and feelings – you say?

Yes, that's an unusual idea for many people. When you ask athletes what they believe psychology can contribute to their performance, many still refer to the standard battery of 'techniques' such as relaxation, visualisation, 'positive thinking' and so on. Many will focus on the importance of identifying negative thinking and replacing it with more positive ideas. Wayne illustrates this in the diagram.

Wayne trying to get past his mind to take a penalty.

Positive thinking might work for some people some of the time, but there are a few things to consider. For example, the 'new' belief must actually be believable. Remember the Brazilian players and their fearful thoughts about the aftermath of the game in the national media. Imagine you had been one of them.

Being positive and telling yourself it won't be so bad has no point; it won't be something you could take on board at that moment. Bad things sometimes do happen, and our mind is completely correct about them. But is there a point in pondering every thought like this and engaging with it? 'One day we all will die' – true enough. What will you do with that thought?

At other times, a thought is not 'true' per se, but – because of the emotional content of our thoughts – things often feel as if they are true. Take this example. 'I made this mistake; I am a loser'. Here, trying to change emotionally-loaded thinking can be an uphill battle.

ACT proposes something new: it says that a thought is just a thought!

And it is not only anxious thoughts that we struggle with: there are also lazy thoughts, and thoughts of worthlessness, amongst many others. Our mind comes up with all sorts of stuff, all the time. Thoughts are sometimes benign, sometimes distressing, and the mind is always busy with something and somewhat distracting, attempting to take us off course.

Thoughts are not always a big problem. It is just that we have a tendency to 'buy in' to some of these thoughts. How do you know you are too focused on certain thoughts? Well, you will feel it. It feels as if the thought has taken over your whole person, as if you are wearing it like a coat or a second skin. Those Brazilian players probably had thoughts like:

'They will ridicule us.'

'We will stay in the Brazil history books forever as a laughing stock.'

'They will never forgive us. I will be remembered as part of the worst Brazilian team ever.'

No positive thinking would have helped them. No amount of relaxation would have helped. Not before, or during the game.

What would have helped?

Not taking their thoughts too seriously, or thinking they meant all that much, might have helped the Brazilian players. Perhaps if they had not given so much attention to losing, and instead used their limited capacity for attention to play to the best of their ability, this might have taken away their fear.

Contrary to common belief, I can actually choose if I want to fully identify with what my mind is telling me. I can choose if I want to believe and buy into everything my mind tells me. I can view my mind's content as 'chit chat' that I simply notice, and can then move on to focus on what needs doing in the real world around me. Actually, this is something we all do all the time. We have thousands of thoughts a day, but only get emotionally hooked on some of them. Those are the thoughts that make us susceptible to fears and anxieties. Many others we forget, because paying no attention means that most thoughts come and go so fast we hardly notice.

For many people, making this switch in how they relate to their mind can be a revelation. The idea that you can have a relationship to your thoughts – or to the mind – and that much of the content is simply chit chat can be a real eye-opener.

What, my thoughts are not reality? They are just ideas?

Yes, really.

Sure, some thoughts are helpful and (more or less) useful representations of the reality we experience as human beings. Words help us to understand the world and allow us to communicate this understanding to others. As a coach, I might say that we are going to practise penalty kicks today, and explain how we do this, and how we can improve on our skills. These are useful ideas that I can communicate to the players.

Words are symbols that stand for something, and they might be more or less useful, or functional, especially if they help you understand what you are going to do in a training session.

The words from the Brazilian public and media however – mocking players during and after the game – were of little use to the Brazilian players. As a player, I wouldn't have wanted to hear these words and the anxiety they would have triggered. Even trying to counter them with others words about relaxing or staying positive would not have helped.

As a player, you are supposed to pay attention to the game you are playing at the time, and not to a conversation in your head! Therefore, trying not to have negative thoughts is not going to work, because it won't help the task at hand.

People sometimes refer to ideas in terms of whether they are 'true' or 'correct'. This, however, is not always what matters in every situation. A thought that this game may be lost in a bad way might be perfectly 'true', but it might not be useful.

Let's go back to the opening example. It was probably correct that the Brazilian public, overall, was condescending towards, and despairing of, their team. Was it helpful though for David Thiago to buy into this thought during the World Cup semi-final? No. Certainly not.

It's a bit like thinking 'I am going die one day' all the time. Even though it is true, does that mean that it's worth pondering it frequently and getting upset?

What if you cannot get rid of a thought?

Try it now! Try not to think of a pink elephant for 30 seconds. What if you tried really hard but the thought hung around? How about thinking positively?

Going with this example, you might try to think of a green elephant instead.

Assume you are successful for a few seconds or longer in getting rid of negative thoughts or the pink elephant. Now picture yourself as a soccer player, on international duty for England, walking up to take your turn in a penalty shootout. You are trying really hard not to think of all sorts of things: the statistics about England in penalty shootouts, your nerves, the English media sharpening their pencils...

And if you somehow manage NOT to think all those things, where do you think your attention has gone? Has it gone to the task, right there in front of you? Probably not.

And that is the problem. The more you engage in these techniques of not having, or not wanting, or trying to replace things in your mind, the more likely you are being taken away from the game you are playing. And that's why many of these traditional strategies simply do not work.

Here is where ACT comes in.

If we can learn to hold a thought more lightly, to just 'look at it' rather than 'from it' (this is something we'll explain in more detail), then we can detach ourselves from this thought to some degree, and it will affect us much less.

An athlete's focus needs to be on the external stimuli of the game, not the internal stimuli of their mind and feelings. Think of attention as a torch in a dark room. A person can shine light internally on themselves, and their thoughts, or externally on what's happening on the playing field around them.

Who this book is for

This book is for coaches and athletes who want to learn a new approach to improved human performance, based on ACT.

The aim of ACT is to help people respond more effectively, and flexibly, to the challenges they meet. The techniques in this book will help you devote more of your attention and energy to what you need to do, whether it is in the midst of competition, or in making sure you train regularly. That is, you will learn to focus on the task at hand rather than to unhelpful, or unimportant internal thoughts. You will learn to respond on the basis of your training, rather than to emotional reactions based on old habits.

Using this book does not require any prior understanding or training of human psychology.

Meet Conradand Wayne

There will be two main characters in this book to help illustrate ideas and concepts.

Wayne, is our first character. He is the clichéd version of an everyday athlete struggling with things. He could be the athlete earning a million dollars, or a weekend player. Wayne tends to get tangled up with his mind and some of its off-topic chatter. He lets his emotions get the better of him at times. He can get really angry, and on occasion becomes so upset that he gets physical and receives a warning.

Conrad, on the other hand, has learned to be less distracted, especially by-passing emotions that don't aid his performance. He is aware of his mind's chatter but if it is not important, or aiding him in the moment, he moves his attention back to the task at hand. When he makes mistakes, he learns from them, rather than beating himself up about 'failure' and catastrophizing about his future. He accepts issues he cannot do much about, like his opponent's great form or the bad weather, and instead spends his energy and time focusing on the one thing he can control... his own performance.

In this book, we will be using Wayne and Conrad as examples of different ways of reacting to, and dealing with, situations.

Onwards!

Chapter 1
What Is ACT?

In this chapter, we will give a brief overview of what ACT is, how it differs from other psychological methods, the key areas ACT addresses, and its relationship to mindfulness.

How the Mind Works

Before we start actively using ACT, it is useful to know about some of the reasons why it works. A lot of the things we are going to suggest go against what people naturally want to do. We are going to suggest – in the right situations – responses like accepting unwanted feelings instead of trying to get rid of them, using less thinking (not more) when dealing with problems of negative thinking, and simply attending to tasks instead of using forced concentration.

ACT is based on an understanding of how human thinking and emotions work. This is informed by a well-supported understanding of human cognition called RFT (Relational Frame Theory). This theory is explained in more detail, next, but the main implication is that it is feelings and emotions that primarily drive and interfere with most of our behaviour. Not so much the ideas or thoughts themselves that run through our heads.

Relational Frame Theory

RFT and other studies of human behaviour have shown us that when we were very young, there was a time when we were not able to think. At least not in terms of words and concepts.

Words and concepts are things you had to learn as a child. Anyone who has brought up a baby, or spent time with very young children, knows that parents spend a lot of time saying things like 'This is Daddy, this is Baby', 'See the kitty', 'Where's Mummy?' What they are doing, in practical terms, is teaching simple types of relationships. You are Baby, I am Daddy. This is Kitty. Kitty is not you. Mummy is somewhere that is not here.

Developmental psychologists have discovered that before we can really learn language, we have to learn these basic relationships; relationships between: here versus there, me versus you, big versus small, good versus bad.

Once we learn to start forming these relationships, complex language really takes off at about 16 months of age. The interesting thing is that we have to learn the difference between here and there, now and then, and we even have to learn the difference between me and you. This understanding is the result of having language.

We do this automatically. What distinguishes us from other creatures is our ability to derive other relationships from the knowledge of a few key relationships. For example, if I tell you that John runs faster than Sam, and Jane runs faster than John – what does that tell you about the relationship between Jane and Sam?

This is not a trick question.

Everyone gets this without having to think about it. In fact, the answer comes up so quickly that most people don't trust themselves and go back and check if they are right. This is an example of how we figure out relationships automatically. We can draw relationships between things we have never seen paired before, and we are the only species on the planet that can do this.

In one experiment, people were taught 19 arbitrary relationships between meaningless symbols. Once they learned these associations (like bigger than, smaller than, worse than, and better than), they could derive 242 different sets of relationships.

We are relationship-generating machines! We can, and do, automatically make judgements, and comparisons, between anything. Good-bad, better-worse, like-don't like.

Now, this can be interesting, but where it gets useful for our purposes is that all words, and concepts, have an emotional component. That is, a physical feeling is attached to them.

While some things feel pretty neutral due to our familiarity with them – a chair, for instance – there is an emotional/somatic tone to words and concepts.

This can be pleasant or unpleasant, depending on experience – our history of learning.

For example, imagine you learn that snakes are dangerous. That is one relationship. Then you learn that snakes live in the grass. What does this tell you about the grass?

Most people will say, 'The grass is dangerous'. Once you have learned these relationships, what feelings will you have if you walk onto, or maybe just think about, the grass? Commonly, this will be fear. A tingling sensation. Perhaps a slight clenching of the throat. A feeling in the stomach. When thinking about this, many people will have an urge to raise their feet up off the ground, presumably to protect themselves from the snakes that aren't there.

The point is that feelings accompany thoughts. Virtually all thoughts. Sometimes they can be very strong, but generally, they are very subtle. It is these feelings that drive our behaviour. Not so much the thoughts themselves.

You might have noticed that people are not like computers in that we don't always react logically to everything, and we don't make well-thought-out, rational decisions each and every time we have to make a choice. We are driven around by our emotional reactions to things. This works out well most of the time, but it can lead to some problems. We can become distressed over things that haven't happened yet, or by things we imagine might happen, or that happened in the past and aren't happening now. This ability to evoke the past and predict the future can be very useful, sometimes. The problem is that if we can't choose when to let these emotions drive us, we are at their mercy, and at the mercy of the various weird and wonderful things our active minds throw up.

The skills that ACT teaches – Openness, Awareness, and Engagement – are all designed to give some choice in when we allow these thoughts, emotions, and bodily sensations to control us, and when we attend to other more pressing issues.

What is ACT?

If you are 'doing ACT', it will look and often feel very different to other psychological approaches.

Instead of trying to control your thoughts, ACT will suggest you don't. Instead of trying to get rid of unwanted and unpleasant emotions, ACT will say 'pay attention' to them. Instead of trying to fix your negative thinking, ACT will say it is fine, just leave it alone. Why? Why is the ACT approach so awkward? Well, really, it isn't. In fact, most people say that once they get the hang of it, ACT feels natural to them. It fits with their experience of what life is like. And it gets results.

So, what is ACT?

ACT is the practical application of the Psychological Flexibility Model. That model says that humans tend to respond to situations in a limited set of ways. We have developed certain patterns of thinking, and sets of standard emotional and behavioural reactions, to most types of situation. This is based on what has worked for us in the past.

The trouble is, the present and the future are not always the same as the past, and we need to be free to respond to changing situations. Part of the reason for this, is that our old patterns of thinking and reacting (both emotionally and behaviourally) can get in the way of effective action. Basically, we tend to be fairly fixed and rigid in our reactions.

A simple example of this would be when you put money in a food or drink vending machine, make your choice, and nothing comes out of the slot.

What do you do?

Most people push the button again. And again. And again.

Sometimes this works, but most of the time, we keep pushing the button long after it is clear we aren't going to get anything. Einstein called this the definition of insanity: doing the same thing over and over and expecting a different result. The behaviour is rigid, and not productive. Developing psychological flexibility means that we can be more creative and responsive to situations that arise.

Emotional reactions can be even more limiting. Imagine our sportsman Wayne, getting feedback from a coach on how to improve a technique. He is very sensitive to criticism. His automatic feeling is that the coach is criticising him. A strong emotional reaction to criticism can lead to old patterns of thinking like: 'They are saying I am rubbish'; 'Everyone will think I am useless'; 'I will get kicked off the team'.

Or, Wayne could react to these emotions by thinking that the coach doesn't know what he is talking about. He might start thinking negative things about his coach, and how he will prove him wrong. In both instances, the player's attention is not fully on the feedback, so he will have missed something that could be helpful to him. Wayne's habitual patterns of thinking and feeling got in the way!

If we are psychologically flexible, we can learn to have these reactions, and still attend to what is happening in the moment. That frees us up to respond on the basis of what is needed, rather than on old emotionally-driven patterns. This suggests that the most effective people are flexible in their response to changing circumstances.

Concisely, the aim of ACT is to help us to become more flexible, accurate, and effective in responding to the situations and the challenges we meet. It is based on an underlying philosophy that puts function – what works – over our ideas and expectations. In psychological terms, that simply means that it puts outcomes over other 'theoretical' considerations such as how we expect things should be, or what we consider to be right or wrong.

ACT also encourages the monitoring of behaviour to see if there is change. With this very functional approach, ACT has identified three broad areas that lead to greater psychological flexibility and effective action. These processes can be summarised roughly as:

1. **Openness** – being open and fully engaged with your own private experiences (feelings, bodily sensations, thoughts)

2. **Awareness** – being aware of the present moment (what is happening now, including what is happening around you), which opens up the opportunity for...

3. **Engagement** – fully committed, effective action, which is based on being fully aware of your personal values (what is important to you)

A strong focus on 'what is fundamentally important to you' is one thing that sets ACT apart from other models of behaviour change. It puts an emphasis on the bigger picture in a way that is relevant to you, the individual, or the team. It puts an emphasis on what works in relation to those things that make what you do worthwhile. Not simply by paying lip service to them, but in a practical, day-to-day manner that relates to what you actually do.

We will describe this in a little more detail shortly, and devote a whole chapter to working with what ACT calls 'Values'. Before we give you a more detailed description of ACT, where it came from, and how it might look in practice, it might be a good idea to first look at what ACT is not. It can be useful to keep this in mind as we work through the exercises in this book.

What ACT isn't

ACT is not a set of techniques.

It is a way of looking at the common basic functions of language and emotion that impede our performance, and provides ways to work with these processes to improve performance.

ACT naturally uses various techniques and strategies, but these are aimed at specific psychological and behavioural processes. We outline these, and how to work with them, in the following chapters. You will be given quite a few strategies and techniques to use. Don't get hung up on individual techniques. Focus on the processes you are working on.

ACT does not supply a recipe book, or cookie-cutter approach. You can use ACT in such a manner – such as designing a set course of interventions for groups – but being aware of the main areas that ACT addresses opens up the possibility of multiple ways of working with the fundamental building blocks of performance (rather than being constrained to a limited range of techniques).

What ACT Is

ACT is a modern form of performance enhancement that developed out of the scientist-practitioner tradition. That means, it is based on science; an understanding of the science of how people work, their feelings, their thinking, and their behaviour. This knowledge is then devoted to practical applications.

ACT is used in a wide variety of settings with the common feature being the development of psychological flexibility as an aid in producing more effective behaviour. While we will talk a lot about emotions, and thoughts, ACT is all about making our behaviour more efficient.

There are a lot of different types of psychology which emphasise slightly different things, or ways of dealing with issues. Often these approaches will emphasise different techniques. The reality is that there are far fewer underlying psychological mechanisms of change, or performance enhancement, than there are techniques or models of change.

If you can identify the psychological mechanisms or areas that are relevant to your situation, you can target them more effectively. That is what we hope to teach you in this book.

ACT and Other Psychological Approaches

ACT differs from its predecessors in the scientist-practitioner tradition in several key ways. For example, from the late 1960s onwards, it was generally assumed that for a person to make changes – whether to improve their performance, deal with anxiety, or other psychological issues – it was necessary to change their thinking. ACT, drawing largely from earlier psychological approaches, questioned whether this was the case.

The first treatment trials of the therapy that eventually became ACT found that it was not necessary to change thinking to help alleviate depression (Zettle & Hayes, 1987; Zettle & Hayes, 1986). This was confirmed by other researchers looking at what was effective in changing behaviour.

Other foundations, or underlying assumptions of ACT, differ from many of its predecessors, and from most other current therapies and performance-enhancement approaches. By analysing the data regarding the nature and prevalence of human suffering, the developers of ACT concluded that experiencing difficulties was not abnormal. ACT took the view, which was a radical departure from the existing thinking at the time, that because you were not happy, not performing well, unsatisfied with your situation, had performance anxiety, were depressed, experiencing substance use problems, or feeling unloved, it did not mean you had a mental illness, that you were defective, had faulty thinking, or were abnormal. It was, in fact, pretty normal. In the words of Psychologist Robyn Walser, 'You aren't broken, you're human'.

This understanding, along with an analysis that examined the way people create greater problems by trying to escape the problems they already have (like trying to stop an emotion, or not having a thought), led to a central concept in ACT – Acceptance. This doesn't mean putting up with things, or just suffering. For ACT, Acceptance means actively grasping your experience; fully living it. This is consistent with the original meaning of the word, actively taking what is offered. It is as if I offered you an apple, and you reached out and took it. Acceptance is actively moving towards, or engaging in, experience rather than finding ways to avoid it, or simply tolerate it. Put simply, Acceptance in ACT means: if you can change things you don't like, do it; if you can't, leave it alone.

Learning acceptance of experience also means learning how not to become overly frustrated, angry, or upset by having experiences that you don't want, and don't like.

As we go through various ways to apply ACT in real-life situations, we will explain these concepts in more detail; however, for the time being, it's useful just to have a simple overview of the main components of ACT. As we said, above, there are three main processes that we target with ACT:

1. Openness
2. Awareness
3. Engagement

We will discuss these ACT processes in more detail in the next chapter and begin to learn how they work by looking at which ones might be most relevant to you. Although working with three processes is really all you need to do, you can break them into six sub-processes:

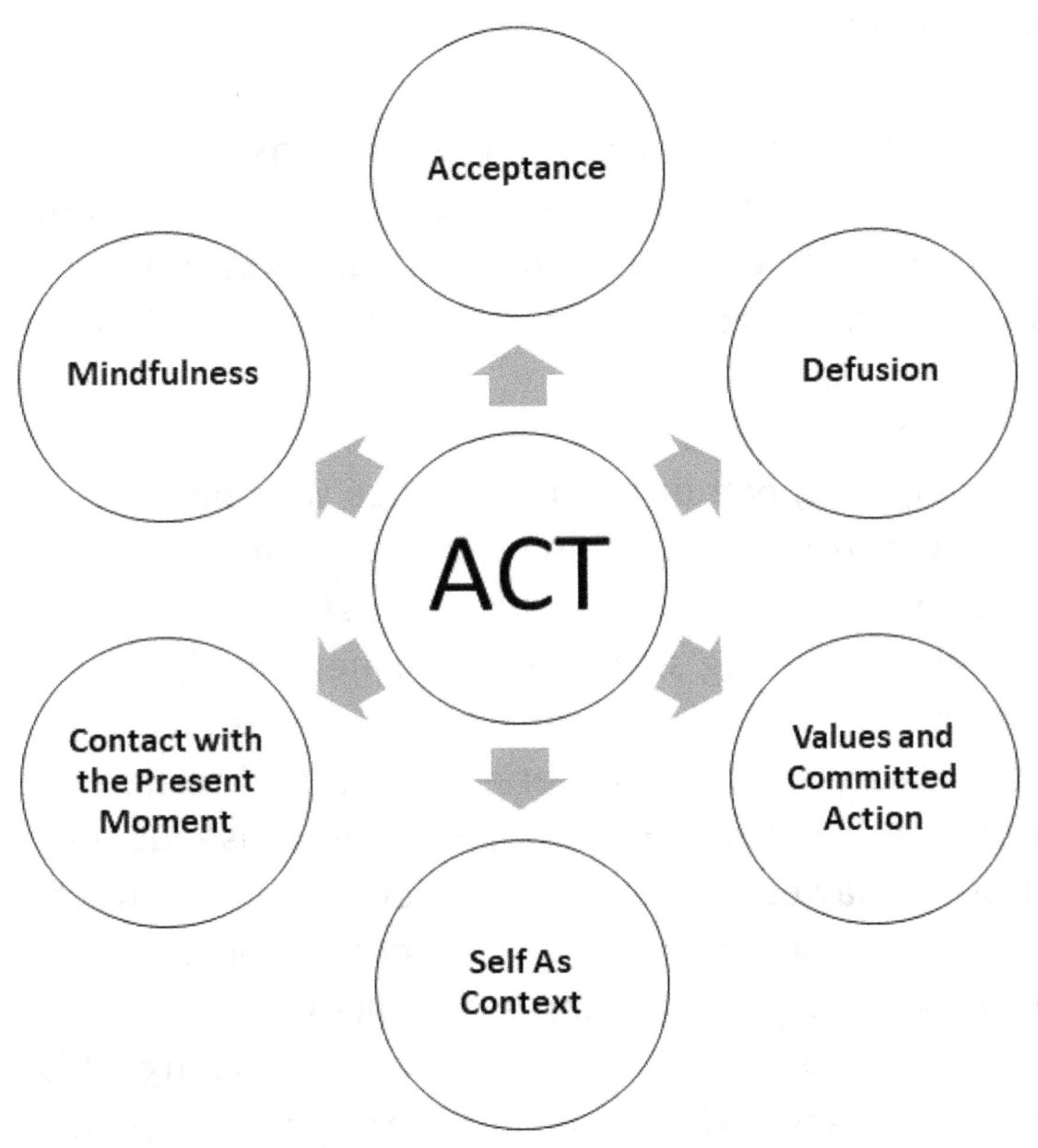

No need to memorise the sub-processes, or feel you must learn them. Just read about them, soak them up, and things will become clearer when we start applying the principles of ACT.

ACCEPTANCE

Acceptance simply means fully embracing, and completely living your experience, both the good and the bad. Not picking and choosing, and not pushing things away. It really does mean embracing all of your experiences.

By doing this, one of the first things we find is ways to stop making the bad any worse than it is (by beating ourselves up mentally, engaging in negative thoughts, avoiding situations, or other unhelpful behaviour). This frees up energy to increase the good, and to learn from our experiences. In ACT terms, that means being directly open to the consequences of our behaviour in the environment, and the direct feedback we are getting. It also means being able to respond regarding what is actually happening, as opposed to 'our ideas' about what is happening. This is a very useful skill for anyone wanting to respond to situations based on their training, and not on their internal state.

Defusion

Defusion is a central idea in ACT, and distinguishes it from other forms of psychology, in that it is based on the understanding that your thinking does not determine your behaviour. In addition, your thinking is not you. Thinking is a tool. Sometimes it is useful; sometimes, it gets in the way.

Basically, from an ACT perspective, your mind is not always your friend. For anyone engaged in sporting endeavours – whether it's golf, running, or any team sport – you will be aware that there are times when your thinking gets in the way of performance.

This is not surprising because this also happens in virtually all other areas of life. We often get all wrapped up in thinking about the situation, our ideas about it, the way different scenarios can play out, the various ways we can mess things up, what different changes in our body mean, and – as a result – our attention and energy get directed or stolen away from the task at hand. Thus, negatively impacting on our performance.

If you have ever drifted off while listening to someone talk, or while reading, you have experienced this. ACT offers a number of ways to focus more on what is happening in the 'here and now' as opposed to what is happening in our heads. One of these ways is to 'defuse' from our thoughts. ACT offers a variety of (what we refer to as) 'defusion techniques'. Simply put, these are ways to not take your thinking so seriously, and to move your attention back to the important aspects of the task at hand.

VALUES AND COMMITTED ACTION

Values and Committed Action are about what is really important to you, and how to make action happen.

Values is a central theme in ACT and, like the term 'acceptance', can have different connotations or meanings to different people.

In ACT terms, values simply mean those things that are, for some reason, very important to you. They are the things that make life worth living. Working with your values is another aspect that separates ACT from other approaches.

For example, if you are a long-term runner and are asked why you like running, you might answer in a lot of different ways. 'I like the competition, I like pushing myself, I like it because I feel good after a run' and so on.

But why do you like competition? Why is pushing yourself good? Couldn't you feel good by having a couple of beers and avoiding the running?

Let's face it, running (biking, swimming, lifting weights, etc.) hurts. Running can be miserable at times, like when it is cold and raining, or too hot. But some people just like it. Why? Because, when you get right down to it, they just do. It gives them something that is generally hard to pin down in words. Something important. It adds something extra, worthwhile, or special to life. Does this mean running is a value for these people? No, running is not the actual 'value' but engaging in physical activity might be.

So, when thinking about values, we might ask: why is your sport, or sport in general, important to you? Why does it matter? How do you want to behave as a sportsperson? What qualities would you like to be remembered as having? These questions are generally not easy to answer. If you have trouble answering, or it takes a while to think about it, engaging in your sport is probably an important value for you. You are not doing it simply to achieve some tangible goal. You just love it!

The problem is that in all areas of life, people tend to get so wrapped up in their goals and how to achieve them that the values – the things the goals are meant to serve – often get lost. An important part of ACT is the identification of values, and the design of 'committed action' towards those values. This generally leads to greater satisfaction, and happiness, in addition to fuelling motivation and freeing up energy to devote to those things that are important to them.

Self As Context

Self As Context (SAC) is the most confusing of the ACT components. For now, all we need to know is that it involves not taking yourself, and your thoughts, so seriously. And believe us, if you are like most people, you probably do, at least on some level.

As an example, often when we have a thought like, 'I am useless', or 'I am no good at this', this becomes our reality. We believe it; even if only for a moment, it feels real. This is self-as-content – seeing (and feeling) that we are exactly and completely what our thoughts are telling us at that moment.

Thoughts, of course, change. At different times, we will have varying levels of belief in any comments we make about ourselves. Realising this, and repeatedly experiencing it, helps us to loosen the hold of a conceptualized self; that is, the unacknowledged ideas we have about who and what we are.

When working with SAC, we practise ways to loosen any rigid beliefs we might have regarding our 'self'; these beliefs get in the way of performance by bypassing our subtle but persistent checking in with our sense of who we are, and how things impact on 'me'. This includes dealing with the deeply-ingrained and automatic assumptions we have that contribute to problems like performance anxiety, or lack of belief in our abilities.

To develop a sense of self that is not simply limited to the ideas in our head, we can practice defusion and acceptance exercises, along with others, that can help us develop a wider perspective. Some ways of doing this include mental exercises like taking other people's points of view, or looking at things from different positions. We can also broaden the boundaries of what we regard as our 'self' through simple physical exercises; all with the view of responding more flexibly, and more immediately, without interference, from unnecessary emotional reactivity. That is, to 'stay in the game'.

SAC exercises are different from cognitive-control strategies like reframing thoughts, or simply trying to learn positive thoughts (affirmations), for the very simple reason that they aim to change our relationship to the thoughts we have, not the thoughts themselves.

This is because practices such as positive thinking, and reframing our thoughts, simply don't work for many of those people who would benefit most from a change in these patterns of thinking.

The thinking, the gut feeling, is so entrenched that hitting it head-on only causes resistance, and an internal fightback. That is why, in SAC exercises, we employ different methods to loosen up the hold of the 'conceptualised self'.

SAC exercises aim to counter the deeply-held, automatic, taken-for-granted views that we have developed around who and what we are. While defusion exercises teach us not to take our thoughts as facts, but simply as passing ideas, SAC exercises teach us not to get tricked into believing thoughts about ourselves.

Ultimately, SAC practices help us become more flexible in response to situations as they arise. We need a conceptualized self in a lot of situations. You need a sense of self to have ambition, for example. Yet, an overactive sense of self in the moment – in the heat of active competition – can be a serious distraction, especially if we start to question ourselves and our abilities. In sport, you need to respond to the current situation in the most flexible and appropriate manner possible. Anything that interferes with that, and with the application of your training, degrades performance and saps energy.

Contact with the Present Moment

A main feature of ACT is being aware of, and responsive to, what is happening around us right now. Not to our ideas about what is happening, or might happen, or what will happen 'if', but to what is actually happening. The idea is simple. By being more switched on to concrete reality, we can respond more flexibly, and effectively.

For ACT, contact with the present moment simply means paying attention to, and having full experience of, what is currently happening. It seems like we do that all the time but, in reality, we are in and out of the present constantly. We are thinking, planning, daydreaming, worrying, running various scenarios in our heads; doing all sorts of things. All good stuff, sometimes.

For optimum performance, contact with what is happening right now is vitally important.

It is like our brain is wired to give us a virtual reality experience most of the time; the only time we are really focused on the moment is when we are highly aroused, often through the fight or flight response.

When we are threatened, we want to run away, or we want to attack. Unfortunately, in those situations, we are so aroused – with our biological systems so stimulated – that our attention and focus narrows. This is good for dealing with a threat or a situation right in front of you, and in some sports where a narrow focus of attention is required, such as in certain shorter swimming events, but we literally lose our wider field of vision; it narrows our attention, and we can make mistakes if we need to shift attention, or modulate our arousal levels.

Being able to switch between a narrow focus of attention and a wider focus is necessary in many sports, and in most areas of life. In addition, this highly aroused state is very time-limited. It doesn't last long. We get burned out very quickly and lose energy. We use contact with present moment practices to develop the skills to increase awareness without depleting our energy resources.

Mindfulness and ACT

In some respects, ACT can be viewed largely as a form of radical mindfulness. Of course, ACT is more than mindfulness, and in turn mindfulness – especially if practiced diligently in traditional forms – is different to ACT. However, it is interesting that researchers, such as Steve Hayes, his colleagues, and other innovators, such as the Psychologist Marsha Linehan, have come to the conclusion that mindfulness is useful in improving people's lives, and in enhancing their ability to deal with difficult, often very stressful, situations.

Many modern therapies and performance enhancement programmes employ various versions, or aspects of mindfulness. ACT is unique among these modern approaches in that it has a very clear definition of what constitutes mindfulness as used within an ACT framework.

For ACT, mindfulness consists of any approach that promotes all of the following: acceptance, defusion, contact with the present moment, and a shift towards experiencing the self as 'self as context' (as opposed to 'self as content').

None of these processes are given greater prominence than another.

Because ACT defines mindfulness as consisting of these four main components, it can provide a variety of mindfulness-type exercises that are not limited to meditation practices. It also means that it is possible to identify specific practices that can suit an individual athlete's, or a team's, needs.

Summary

- ACT aims to improve function – towards what is valued – by targeting three broad psychological processes. For use in practice, we have called these: Openness, Awareness, and Engagement.

- These processes consist of six main components or sub-processes: Acceptance, Defusion, Contact with the Present Moment, Self As Context (SAC), Values, and Committed Action.

- This book will be most useful to you if you treat it as a workbook, and use the exercises to identify your particular needs, and then apply ACT processes and exercises to your situation. To help with this, we will provide a variety of exercises you can use.

- To get the most out of the book – be consistent, and do the exercises.

- While the focus of this book is on applying ACT to sport, it will help you deal with any barriers you have to living the life you want. It has been our experience that you can't separate life and sport, and that you will likely find the issues/habits/attitudes relating to your sporting performance also relevant to other areas of your life.

Have fun, and good luck!

Chapter 2
THE THREE PILLARS

In the previous chapter, we talked about ACT and the various components that make up the ACT approach to improving performance: acceptance, defusion, present moment awareness, self as context, values, and committed action. These can seem quite confusing; the words are strange, the concepts are new, and all these aspects of ACT seem to interact or overlap with each other to some extent. If you look at the following diagram, you'll see that the various components of ACT are laid out in a way that shows that they are connected.

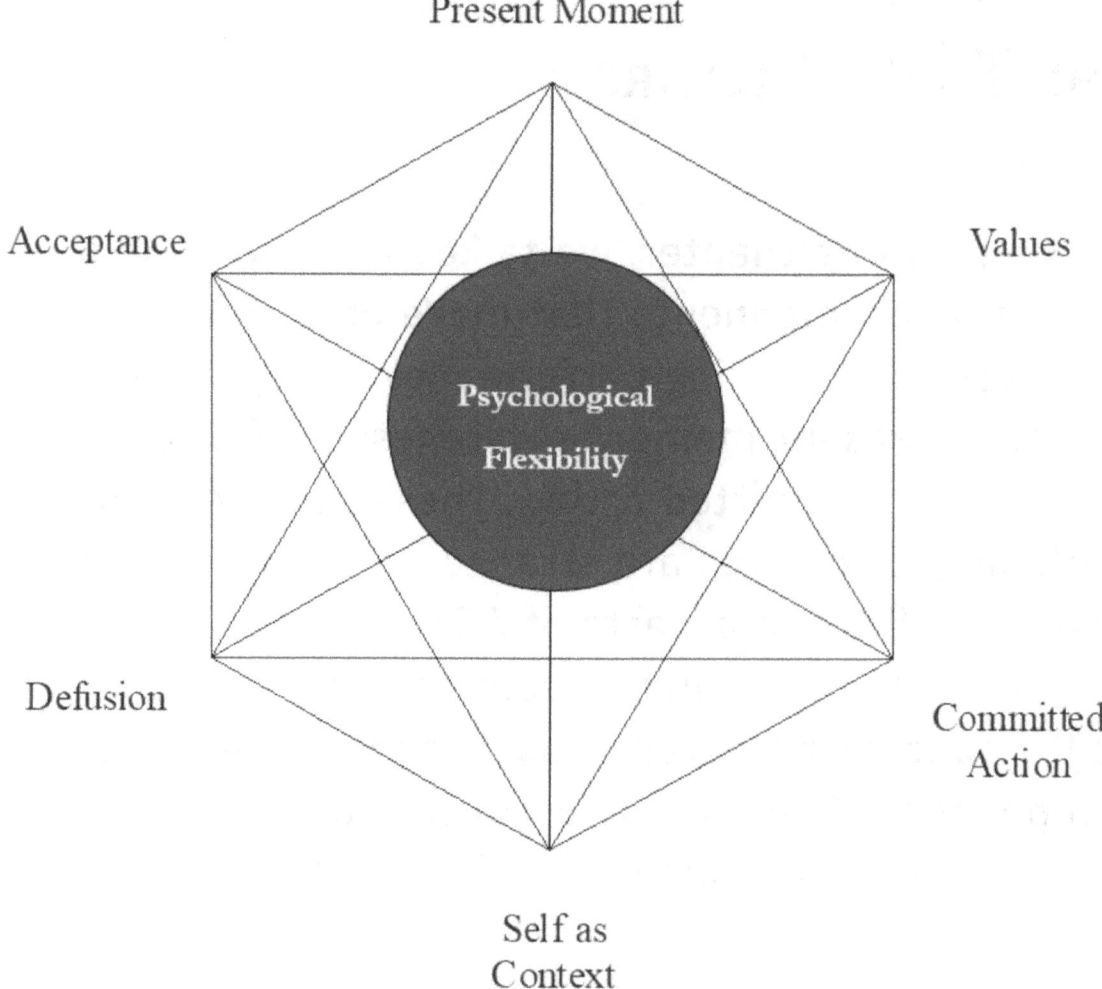

[Copyright Steven C. Hayes. Used with permission.]

At the centre of the diagram is what ACT aims to develop, namely 'Psychological Flexibility'. This is simply the ability to respond in an adaptive, flexible, and effective manner to changing situations. It means doing away with any unnecessary hindrances caused by unhelpful emotional reactivity, rigid thinking, and old ineffective habits of behaviour.

This is a well-known diagram which appears in many books on ACT, but it has a lot going on in it. A much simpler way of looking at it, is to look at the three columns of the diagram and think about the activities, or processes they represent. Kirk Strosahl has referred to these more general processes as **Openness**, **Awareness**, and **Engagement** (Strosahl, Robinson, & Gustavsson, 2012).

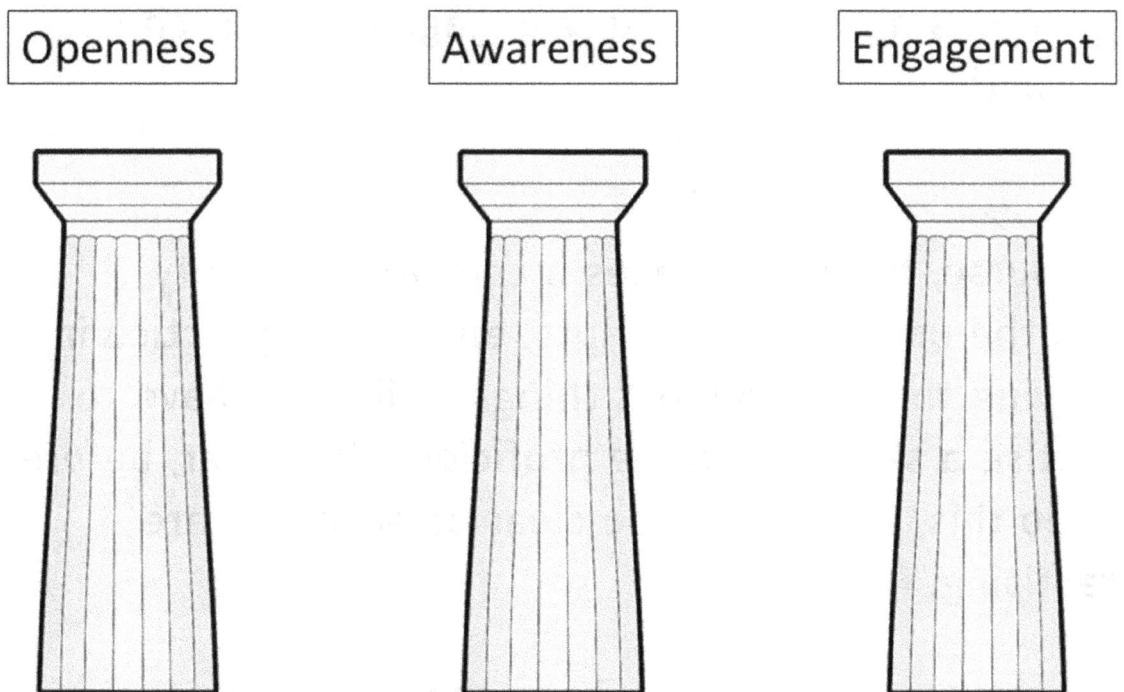

This is a very useful way of looking at the ACT processes. In practice, it is much more user-friendly, especially when you are first learning the skills. Instead of having to mentally check each of the six processes outlined in the more complex diagram (to see if I am accepting, defusing, fully present, and so on) it is much easier to think about checking in to:

1. Being open to internal experience
2. Aware of what's happening in and around you
3. Focusing on being fully engaged in your chosen activity

Of course, to do this takes a certain familiarity with the underlying concepts, and actual practice in applying them. Like most things in life, we have to practise a skill to become proficient. However, before we do this, we need to be clear on what we are practising.

Openness: This refers to the ability to be fully aware of, and not reject, unwanted internal physical and emotional experiences. These can include pain, self-doubt, distracting thoughts, fear, embarrassment, and so on. As you might have noticed, this process includes the ability to avoid getting wrapped up in our thoughts, worries, unwanted feelings, and fears – to the extent that they distract us from what is important. Openness incorporates acceptance and defusion.

Awareness: This involves contact with the present moment, what is happening around us right now, the physical reality outside the skin, in addition to what is going on in our body; and what might be best-called defusion from our self-concept. This just means not being ruled by old ideas about ourselves and our abilities. Not taking ourselves too seriously, and reducing the need to protect our self-esteem (self as context).

Developing a sense of self as context might show itself as listening to criticism, judging it honestly, and not getting angry or defensive about it; or, when a mistake is made, choosing to learn from it without beating yourself up. If we are completely involved or taken up with what we are doing, there is no concern with our self-concept or our self-esteem. We are simply aware of what's happening, and fully engaged in that activity. We are focused more on the external environment, and the task at hand, rather than the internal environment (thoughts and emotions). With this type of awareness, we don't try to exclude internal experience; it is simply not given priority, or a lot of our attention. We are more fully aware of what we see, feel, hear, and touch.

The lack of priority given to self-esteem, or self-concept, does have an important function at times. In those moments of 'flow' (Csikszentmihalyi, 2008), when everything just clicks, and we perform a technique perfectly, there is no idea of self, no self-referencing. At least not until immediately after the event. Then we feel pretty good about ourselves because things have gone well. At the time, any thoughts of 'self', 'me', 'how I am doing', 'how I might look to others', and 'what if I look stupid' are simply not there. If they were, they would get in the way. Imagine stepping up to the free-throw line in basketball in front of all the players of both teams, a crowd of spectators, and feeling like you will be judged and blamed if you miss. Paying too much attention to thoughts like this, and the emotions that go with them, can certainly interfere with your performance.

Engagement: Engagement means not only being fully involved in what you are doing but being involved because it is important to you, because – at heart – it is what you want to be doing. For example, there are two ways to go to practice; you do it because you have to, and as a result tend to go through the motions, or you do it because it is part of your broader values (you see it as important or meaningful). The second approach leads to more active participation. You pay more attention and put more effort in because it is in line with what is important to you. No one can decide what is meaningful for you. Some reasons why going to training might be important could be wanting to improve your performance, or because you have made a commitment to the team, or the coach. The specific value doesn't matter. Engagement is being clear about what your values are, and then acting on them (Committed Action). You do this even when it is difficult, or you don't feel like it. You do it even if you falter, or fail, and have to start again.

The Three Pillars in Action

In using ACT to improve performance, intellectual knowledge can be helpful, but the only way you can really develop practical skills is to practise. That is why – throughout this book – we are going to ask you to do exercises, engage in practice activities, and to write things down. This is important. To understand ACT, you have to do it.

The first thing we are going to do is to develop a working knowledge of the Three Pillars, the core processes of ACT.

Here are some examples of common ways people react to certain situations. By looking through these examples, and by answering a few questions about them, you will become more familiar with the various components of ACT. You will also become familiar with common patterns of behaviour that impede performance. This will make it easier for you to spot your own unhelpful tendencies, and to apply the techniques suggested in the rest of this book.

For the examples below, try to see which behaviours are the most open, aware, and engaged. This is good practice for noticing when you might be closed off, are avoiding things, disengaged, or wrapped up in your own thoughts.

Situation	Behaviour 1	Behaviour 2	Behaviour 3
A. Feeling nervous at the start of a match: funny feeling in stomach, throat tight	Talking about something other than the game. Distracting yourself by looking around at the spectators. Thinking about what you will do after the match.	Thinking 'I hate this,' 'I am going to be sick.' 'This will be a disaster,' 'I hope I don't f#@k up.'	Noticing feelings in the stomach, noticing the wind on your face, the grass. Aware of thoughts but not maintaining them by dwelling on them. Focusing on your warm up.

Situation	Behaviour 1	Behaviour 2	Behaviour 3
B. Not wanting to go to practice, feeling tired.	Staying home and playing PlayStation.	Giving yourself reasons why you shouldn't go. 'I'm tired,' 'I think I am getting a cold,' 'I will avoid injury if I don't go when I am not 100%,' 'I need to spend time with family,' 'I'll perform better when rested.'	Feeling where the tiredness is in the body. Noticing what it feels like. Awareness of thoughts about staying home and focusing on getting your gear to go to training.

Situation	Behaviour 1	Behaviour 2	Behaviour 3
C. Getting annoyed with something your coach, or one of your training partners/ teammates has said to you, and not attending to what the coach is saying right now.	Re-focusing on what the coach is saying. Even asking them to repeat something you missed.	Drifting off and thinking about something else.	Mentally listing reasons why they are wrong, or how unfair what they said is. Or, thinking something along the lines of what an idiot they are.

Now, get a piece of paper and a pen or pencil. In this exercise, we are going to ask a couple of questions about these behaviours and ways of reacting.

SITUATION A – FEELING NERVOUS

Make a heading on your sheet of paper – Situation A – and write down the behaviour number (e.g., 1, 2 or 3, from the table above) that relates best to the response you experience. Now, answer the following:

1. In situation A, which way of reacting to the situation is most open and engaged?

2. Which reaction is most avoidant, where the individual tries not to feel the emotions, or to think about it?

3. In which one is the person most wrapped up in their thoughts, and considerations about themselves?

Now check your answers against ours, and check our reasoning.

For Situation A, Behaviour 3 is the most open and engaged. The person is attending to the actual physical reality around them, and to their feelings and bodily sensations. In addition, they are not letting these thoughts and feelings drag them off task into some internal self-talk and away from what is happening. If we look at their behaviour – what they actually do – they are focusing on their warm up. Something related to their goal.

If we look at what the person did in Behaviour 1, on the other hand, we can see that they are clearly avoiding their uncomfortable thoughts and feelings by distracting themselves. They are mentally getting out of the situation, using any tactic they can: looking around, thinking of other things. They are clearly not open to their immediate experiences.

Behaviour 2 is also not open, or aware. The person is more wrapped up in thinking related to themselves. They appear 'fused' with their thoughts. It is all about 'me', and quite negative. This is the type of thinking that is likely to wind someone up and make them feel worse. Now remember, in ACT we want psychological flexibility. We don't want to eliminate, or avoid, certain thoughts. We just don't want to feed them or keep them going if they are not helpful. The response in column three (Behaviour 3) gives an idea of how to do this. Feel the feelings, have the thoughts, and simply keep doing what you need to do and pay attention to that. This is where mindfulness practice is helpful. It trains us to more easily, very gently, to shift attention to where it needs to be without undue effort or stress. We will talk more about how to do that later.

SITUATION B – NOT WANTING TO GO TO PRACTICE

Let's look at situation B. Not wanting to go to practice is something most people have probably experienced at some stage.

1. On your piece of paper, under the heading Situation B, write the number of the behaviour that represents the most open, aware, and engaged response to the situation.

2. When you have done that, explain why this response is the best fit. Write it down. What is the person open to? What are they not avoiding? What are they aware of? What is their behaviour

focused on? That is, if we had a video camera on them – what would we see and hear?

3. In which response (Behaviour 1, 2, or 3) is the person wrapped up in their thoughts, or involved in 'reason giving'? In which response are they avoidant? What do you think they might be avoiding about training? Now, write your responses down. This makes it real (not just ideas in your head that you can skip over and almost ignore). Also, be sure to add anything extra you can think of, like why they might want to avoid training, by using your own experience.

As in the first example, Behaviour 3 represents the most open, aware, and engaged response to feeling like missing training. The person not only engages in behaviour towards their goals (getting their training gear and going), they also make themselves open to feelings of tiredness, thoughts of not wanting to go, and the desire to avoid training today. They don't dwell on them. They don't engage in any kind of internal debate, or commentary, either. They feel it, they think it, and they move on towards what they need to do.

Behaviour 1 is straight-out avoidance. Not only does the person not go to training, but they do something else so they don't even think about it, or much of anything else. They veg out with a computer game. Which is fine, of course, as long as it does not interfere with things that are important to them.

Behaviour 2 represents getting wrapped up in an internal conversation, and reason giving. Giving reasons for not doing something that you have already decided (committed) to do, but you don't feel like now is – for a short time at least – a sure sign of avoidance. Catching ourselves getting caught up in 'reason giving' can be a clue as to when we are moving away from being engaged, or doing things consistent with what is important to us. In those situations where we have already made a commitment to do something we find important or meaningful, reason giving can be a clue that we are:

1. Not open
2. Not aware
3. Not engaged

Thinking things through, and problem-solving, are obviously important in the right situations. But, when we are about to wash the dishes, brush our teeth, pay a bill, or go to training, and we start thinking through reasons why we will do it later, it is probably a sign that we are simply avoiding things. It is a signal that we are disengaging; shying away from important parts of our life.

SITUATION C – GETTING ANNOYED

Thinking of the Three Pillars (Openness, Awareness, Engagement), and the ACT principles underlying them, write down what is happening (for Situation C) in Behaviour 1, just like we did for the other two situations. Do the same thing for Behaviours 2 and 3. Think things through by imagining you are in that situation, and doing those things, such as drifting off. How would that be described by ACT? Take your time and do a good job on this.

We are not going to give you our ideas for this situation. This is up to you to think about. This is not so much about getting a 'right' answer, but about thoroughly investigating the situation, and becoming familiar with what is a flexible, useful way of dealing with thoughts and feelings.

For example, if you were in this situation, how would it feel to ask the coach to repeat themselves in a team meeting? Would this be easy to do? Would it be embarrassing? What would be the point of it?

In the examples above, we haven't focused on what drives a person to do something. Often, this can be vague and hard-to-define. That is because each of us has slightly different set of things that are important to us (values in ACT terms). Because there are variations in what drives us, and what is meaningful for us, it is important that you identify your own values. We will focus on that in the next chapter. For now, however, let's focus on barriers to success.

Identifying Your Barriers to Performance: Step 1

If you bought this book, it is likely you have some ideas about what you find difficult, or what you want to improve. For some people, anxiety or stress gets in the way of performance. A lack of confidence, or negative self-talk, and self-doubt, is a problem for other people. For others, it can be a lack of commitment to, or the regularity of, training.

Think about what you struggle with, and what brought you to buy this book, and write that down. Try to be as specific as possible. Try writing 'I struggle with ...', or 'I find ... hard because ... ', or 'I lack ...' and fill in the blanks. If possible, give several examples of when you have felt this was a problem.

If you can, write down a feeling in your body that comes along with your self-identified barrier or difficulty, and at least one thought that also arises. This can be hard. That is normal, and if you can't identify any bodily sensations, or thoughts, at this stage, it's all right.

A lot of people are tempted not to write things down, especially if they already have an idea about what they struggle with. Their reasoning often goes something like, 'I already know it. I've thought about it already. No need to write it down', even 'I don't want to go get a pen'. Seems reasonable. However, the experience of writing things down is different to just thinking about things. It is more real. We feel it more emotionally, and physically. Sometimes quite strongly. The reason we don't want to write things down is not just laziness on our part, or impatience and wanting to move on to the next section of the book – it is because it is uncomfortable. Maybe only very slightly, like having to find a pen, but it is uncomfortable. This is emotional avoidance.

This is the core of what we are dealing with.

The often subtle, hard-to-detect, attempts to avoid what we don't want that can get in the way of performance. So, when we ask you to write something down, please do it. Our experience is that reading a book like this can be interesting, but it won't change much. What changes behaviour is doing things. It is practice.

Once you have written down what you struggle with, think of the times this has been more of a problem than others. Think of three times that spring to mind, or stand out. Write them down. Then list some examples when this hasn't been such a problem, or even not there at all. Have you noticed any common factors or triggers that make things worse, or make them better? If so, write them down. Something along the lines of 'When. . . I struggle with (or have. . .). . .', 'When. . . things seem better'.

Your responses might look something like this.

What do I struggle with?

- I hate playing in front of a crowd.
- I get nervous and make stupid mistakes in a game.
- I don't want to feel like a loser.

What I feel

- I feel sick in my stomach.
- I get sweaty.

What I think

- I have thoughts like, everyone is looking at me.
- They think I am crap and shouldn't be playing.

When is it bad?

- This happened for each of the last three games we had.

When is it better?

- It didn't happen the first game this season.

Triggers or signs for the worst.

- The bigger the ground, the bigger the crowd, the better the competition, the worse I feel.

Triggers or signs for the better

- I felt really relaxed and fit for the first game, and there was hardly anyone there watching.

If you can't put something under every heading, that is ok. Just do your best. Some people find it very hard to identify their triggers. Others find it difficult to identify feelings or thoughts. Take your time and think through the different situations you have been in; see if you can put something under each of the headings above.

Now, think of the different ACT processes we have talked about (see the diagram at the start of this chapter), and the Three Pillars. List the areas you think you might need to work on most. Is it being more Open, Aware, or Engaged? Write down the main areas you think you need to work on, and you can pay particular attention to them as we work through the book.

For practice, you can look at the example immediately above, and write down what that person might want to avoid. Is it the crowd? Is it the game? Or is it their feelings? What do you think would be useful for them to work on in terms of the Three Pillars?

Further on is a list of some common issues and behaviours people face, and the skills that help in dealing with them. We have listed the main core skills and the general process, or attitude, from the Three Pillars that most often apply. See if any always apply to you. If so, write them down; and, on your piece of paper, write down others that sometimes apply to you. Write down all the areas you think you need to work on.

You will see that we have listed several areas of skill development for each type of behaviour. This is partly because these skills overlap to some extent. The other reason is that, for some people, one type of skill will be more important than for another person with the same general issue. So, attention towards your own situation, your own experience, and your triggers is important. It helps you to be more specific about what to work on.

Behaviour	Area of Skill Development – From the Three Pillars
Spend a lot of time criticising yourself	Open, Aware (e.g., defusion, acceptance, self as context)
Spend a lot of time feeling anxious	Open, Engaged (e.g., acceptance, defusion, committed action)
Avoid situations, tasks, (procrastination) etc.	Engaged, Open (e.g., committed action, values, acceptance, maybe defusion)
Comparing yourself to others	Open, Aware (e.g., defusion, self as context, acceptance)
Choking when you need to perform	Aware, Open, Engaged (e.g. present moment, acceptance, defusion, committed action)
Lack of confidence	Open, Aware, Engaged (e.g., defusion, acceptance, self as context, values, and committed action)

Behaviour	Area of Skill Development – From the Three Pillars
Not fully committed in training, or in competition	Engaged, Open, Aware (e.g., values clarification, committed action – possibly also defusion, present moment awareness, and self as context depending on what is driving the lack of commitment)
Losing focus in training or competition (drifting off)	Aware, Engaged (e.g., Present moment awareness, committed action)

Consider what we have done so far as a work in progress. We are going to continue to look at identifying barriers to performance as we move through this book and work with different problems. One very powerful way is to simply be aware of, and briefly record, your reactions in different situations. Take note of what triggers avoidance, an internal struggle or resistance, or what creates discomfort for you. What do you do when that happens? How do you shift your attention away from your most valued activities? This process is a very important tool in developing awareness.

Once we have an enhanced awareness of how we react, what we do, and how our thinking changes – we then have the opportunity to catch those processes earlier, and step out of automatic mode. It is only then that we can practise moving our attention back to where we want it. Basically, we are learning how to step away from old habits. Old habits of reacting emotionally, physically, behaviourally, and in our thinking.

Learning to be more aware can be harder than it seems. Not because it is necessarily a difficult skill to learn; it is just that we like to do things on auto-pilot, and learning any new skill takes effort. We have provided a record sheet for you to download. The key thing here is to use it and to write things down.

How to use the record sheet

On the sheet provided, you will see four columns – Situation, Bodily Sensations, Thoughts, Behaviour. The first column is for the situation you find yourself in, and the date. All you need is a few words to help you remember the situation. For example, going to training/Friday. The second column is for bodily sensations. That is any physical sensation you feel in your body. That can be heat or warmth, cold, tingling, the wind on your skin, anything at all. You don't have to write a lot in any of these columns but it is crucial to be as specific as possible. For example, tingling in hands, or a warm tingling in hands could both be good descriptions. As would tightness in throat, warm stomach. The third column shows a thought bubble. This column is for anything that you might think; anything that pops into your head. These can be thoughts, images, or your judgements and evaluations about things. It can also be picturing things you want to say or do.

A useful way to go about filling in the sheet is to think of a situation shortly after it happens, or later in the same day. Then, mentally walk through what happened; like you are re-living it in your imagination. Then, notice what sensations you have (or had) in your body, and what thoughts came up. Try to be as specific as possible.

The fourth column is for recording your behaviour. What you did. That is anything that would be seen if someone had a camera on you and was recording a video. Write down anything that can be seen or heard. Again, be specific. Some examples might be clenching your fist, frowning, hitting something, walking away, even clenching your jaw, or rolling your eyes. You can be brief; use just a few words. You don't have to write a story about it, or even use real sentences. Just a few words describing what you felt, thought, and did. By paying attention to our reactions in this way, we develop much more awareness of what's happening in our bodies, what is happening in our minds, and even of what we do.

It is helpful to complete at least two or three examples a day. It's useful if you can pick things that are related to what you struggle with, or what creates difficulties for you. Examples might be tension, anxiety, putting things off, a lack of confidence, and so on. You can also practice by using just small everyday things. In fact, it is good to include a range of things. For example, if you make a cup of coffee and it gets cold before you get a chance to drink it, record your reaction. Or, if you are going somewhere and get held up in traffic, record how you feel, where you feel it, and what goes through your head. Include what someone who was watching very closely would see and hear. These are all useful ways of developing the ability to attend to your body, thoughts, and behaviours. As we progress through the book, we will develop these abilities and use them in dealing with barriers to performance.

EMOTIONS

You might have noticed that we have not specifically asked you to record emotions. To paraphrase Tina Turner, 'What's emotion got to do with it?' We will talk about emotions in more detail when looking at how to deal with things like anxiety, anger, fear of failure, sadness, and frustration. However, by filling out the record sheet, you will already be covering emotions. When you look at emotions closely, they are simply bodily reactions (sensations), accompanied by certain types of thoughts, and actions. If you are recording feeling angry, for instance, the word anger tells us how you feel, but it is not specific enough for us to work with, at least not effectively. What we need to be aware of is what you feel in your body when you are angry. What goes through your head, and what you do.

Wayne, might fill out something like the example below.

Situation & Day	Bodily Sensations	Thoughts/ Images/ Evaluations	Behaviour (What a video camera would see and hear)
Kicked from behind when running with the ball. Thur.	Pain in back of calf – sharp, hard. Hot face, tight fists, burning jolt in stomach	B*&^$d! You #@%&! I'm gonna get you. Image/ visualise punching opponent	Angry face, clenched fists, getting up off ground. Turns and shouts at opponent.

As we have said, previously, practicing noticing your automatic reactions, and writing them down is an important exercise. This is one way of helping you to understand what difficulties you are facing and gives a good sense of what you might want to work on. We won't ask you to do this forever but, for now, it is a very good foundational practice that we can build on as we work with various ACT processes in the following chapters.

Another practice that will help with this self-analysis, and in developing most ACT-related skills and psychological flexibility, is mindfulness.

Mindfulness

Many popular books on athletic performance and peak performance, from The Inner Game of Tennis (1974) to Mihaly Csikszentmihalyi's Flow (2008) have commented on the state where the athlete, or the performer, finds themselves in an almost magical condition where everything just clicks into position, and things happen perfectly. This same state is often depicted in action films, especially martial arts films, where the hero – in a state of almost detached awareness – manages to overcome insurmountable odds by applying the skills they have learned over many years.

Now, this can seem a little bit unrealistic, but many people do indeed experience a state of flow. There are those moments when things seem to go perfectly. Where you are just there, on point, and there is nothing but the performance.

Surfers talk about this when describing riding a tube.

You don't have to be an elite athlete to experience this. It is common for all types of sportspeople to talk about that moment when everything just clicks. It can be hitting the sweet spot when batting, or performing an excellently-timed tackle in football. Anything at all where a much better than expected reaction is driven solely by instinct and training – without you consciously co-ordinating the action. These moments are basically what athletes train for; to be able to perform at the peak of their abilities without interference from internal or external distractions.

The things we talk about in this book are all aimed at helping us to perform better. Mindfulness is one of the tools we can use to do this. We have alluded elsewhere that there are different forms of mindfulness, and different therapies and schools of thought that tend to use mindfulness in slightly different ways. For our purposes, we use mindfulness based on both our understanding of ACT, and our understanding of meditation techniques.

For us, and as it's presented in this book for your use, mindfulness is an experiential process. It is mainly a body-based exercise. It is an activity. It is something you do. It is not an intellectual exercise. It is not about thinking. It is not about not thinking. It is about being.

It is fully experiencing your life without any conceptual overlay. That is, without thought getting in the way; without adding interpretation to your experience. That is what the ideal is, anyway.

As an example of adding interpretation to your experience, imagine walking out on a cold damp morning and thinking about how cold it is, how you hate this weather, and how you wished it wasn't so far to your car. The alternative is simply being aware of the cold: the tingle on your skin, the breeze, the way your breath moves like clouds in the air. Simply experiencing 'what is' without adding to it. We will give you some exercises you can use to help develop mindfulness, and the ability to act more flexibly to changing circumstances.

One exercise that can demonstrate the way the mind wanders, jumps around, and doesn't do what it is told, is what we call the finger exercise.

> **The Finger Exercise**
>
> Get comfortable. Wiggle around if you need to loosen up, then sit up straight in a chair, let your shoulders drop and relax a little. We are going to ask you to close your eyes and allow yourself to breathe calmly and gently. Then put the forefinger of your right hand on your right thigh, about halfway between your knee and hip. Simply hold it there, and pay attention to your breath as you breathe in and breathe out. There is no need to control your breathing, just be aware of it.
>
> That's all you have to do, except if you notice yourself thinking about something other than

your breathing. If you notice your thinking going to something in the past, pull your finger back towards your hip. If you find it on something to do with the future, move it towards the knee. When you are just attending to your breathing, move it back to the middle. Do this for three to five minutes. Make sure you time it. Sit, breathe, and be aware of your breathing. Move your finger depending on where the thoughts that pop into your head go.

Review

What did you notice while you were doing the finger exercise? Did you just sit and pay attention to your breathing with a blank mind? Did thoughts pop up on their own? Did they move back and forth between the past and the future? Were they all about the present?

Most people find that their minds throw up quite a few thoughts, images, worries, and plans. All sorts of things can come up in relatively quick succession, and this happens whenever we just sit and attend to something simple. These small but fairly constant lapses in attention, and moments

> of distraction, are perfectly normal. However, when we are trying to perform at a high level, and need to react immediately and efficiently, distractibility – even for a split second – can be counter-productive. What are normal lapses in attention or intention for most of us, and slight delays in responding, can lead to mistakes and errors not only in high-performance situations, but in any athletic activity.

Among the skills that we will train in developing psychological flexibility with ACT is how to increase openness and awareness to what's actually happening in the world outside our skin, rather than overly focusing on what is happening internally. We develop the ability for our attention to become more stable, and less susceptible, to all the various distractions that our habitual ways of thinking and feeling throw at us. When we are less reactive to unbidden or automatic internal events, we can respond more effectively in the present, physical reality – like when a ball is coming towards us, or when another athlete is making a break.

The above exercise helps show how our minds work. We can see that we are not always in control of our inner processes. In fact, our minds (our patterns of thinking) seem to have minds of their own. Once we have noticed some of these tendencies, the next step is to start to do something about it. You have been given some tools to begin improving your ability to notice patterns of reacting in the record sheets you were asked to fill out. Now we are going to look at a practice that helps make us more aware, more focused, and better able to deal with distractions.

MINDFULNESS OF BREATH

The granddaddy of all mindfulness exercises, the one that all others are derived from, is mindfulness of breath. This is a practice that really develops the mindfulness/awareness muscles. It is so effective because it requires direct contact with actual physical experience. It also requires 'open consent,' an allowing of this experience. As a result, it helps build attention to what is going on, in addition to developing openness and awareness skills. It also requires engagement. For our purposes, there is no better exercise than mindfulness of breath in building openness, awareness, and engagement.

The 'idea' of mindfulness of breath can seem quite simple. In reality, it can be a difficult exercise. It is by no means a beginner's exercise in the sense you need to move on from it to something more complicated. People who have practiced meditation for decades still practise mindfulness of breath, and mindfulness of the body.

It trains openness, awareness, and engagement by getting in touch with what is happening in physical reality, rather than what is going on in our thoughts and imagination, when (at least at times) we would rather be doing something else.

With mindfulness practice, you are effectively turning down the volume of the verbal part of the brain, and turning up the part that deals with somatic, or physical sensations. Studies of those with a history of practicing mindfulness show an association with a larger somatosensory cortex. That is the part of the brain that has the main responsibility for awareness of physical sensations in the body. There have also been studies that have shown changes (enlargements) in some parts of the frontal cortex associated with the ability to attend. In other words, if you practice mindfulness regularly, it changes your brain. This shouldn't be surprising. It is a skill, and a developmental exercise. In a way, it is like push-ups for the mind. The more you do, the better you get.

How to do it

The simple answer, and the most practical is, find a relatively quiet place where you are unlikely to be disturbed. Get into a stable and comfortable upright position. Then pay attention to the physical sensations of breathing. That's it!

Below are some simple instructions on how to practise.

> **Posture in mindfulness practice**
>
> Mindfulness practice is about being awake and aware, while not responding to (or engaging in) unnecessary thought. We achieve this by taking an upright, relaxed, and open posture while we practice. Sitting upright is important because

it helps us to stay alert. When we slouch or lie down, we are more likely to drift off, daydream, or fall asleep, simply because that is what we often do when we are in those postures.

Some people like to practice mindfulness while lying in bed and it is, of course, possible to be mindful while lying down or slouching on the couch. Or even while sprinting! The problem is that maintaining an alert, open, aware attitude is more difficult under these circumstances. Even when you are experienced at mindfulness practice, it is important to minimise distractions and to use whatever tools you can to remain relaxed, yet alert and attentive.

We think of the attitude we take in mindfulness practice as similar to the type of awareness you might have if you think you have heard the faint ringing of a phone and are simply listening. Not straining, not tense, just aware and open to what might be there. That attitude is reflected in an upright posture.

If you are going to sit and practice mindfulness for more than five or ten minutes, it's good to have your hips higher than your knees. If you don't, the effect is to subtly throw your chin forward, which eventually causes tension, and pain in the neck and back. This is one of the main reasons meditators traditionally sit cross-legged on a cushion on the floor. It's not that they didn't have chairs in the past, or that there is something mystical about that posture. In that position, your bum is raised above your hips, your spine is relatively straight and upright, and your legs serve to balance you. Believe it or not, for most people this is the most comfortable position when sitting still for long periods. In this position, provided you allow your body to relax slightly, you use the minimal amount of muscle tension necessary to remain upright and alert. Though we admit it does take some getting used to.

You can achieve the same posture by sitting on a chair with a cushion or a blanket on it to raise your bottom, or by sitting on the edge of your bed with your legs slightly bent. Having said all that, what really matters is doing what works for you! We encourage you to experiment a little bit, but not to change posture during a practice session unless it feels like you are actually hurting yourself.

If you do decide to sit cross-legged, it is generally best to have one leg bent in front of the other (called The Burmese Position), not on top of each other as this will cause pain. It can also be hard on the knees to keep them bent at an extreme angle for long periods. Unless you are very flexible, your knees won't touch the ground. In that case, get something like a towel, or a small cushion, to rest your knee or lower leg on. Pretty much anything will do. We have even used running shoes. This support will reduce discomfort by supporting your legs, and keep you balanced.

Instructions

Be aware of the feeling of the breath in the body as you breathe in and breathe out. All you have to do is be aware. Now, if you are like most people, your attention will be pulled in different directions. As discussed in the exercises above, thoughts, feelings, urges to move, plans for the future, memories, all sorts of things come up. This is ok. That is what happens. It's not wrong. Your job in practising mindfulness is simply to become aware of the sensations of breathing wherever they are occurring at the time. It helps to not make anything – and I do mean anything – of what we think of as distractions; the other things that come up. In this exercise, in this practice, we are learning to attend to what is physically happening, and not so much to our thoughts and fantasies about what is happening, should happen, did happen, or might happen. It's about fully experiencing what is happening now. Fully allowing it.

So, when you start judging how you are doing, thinking of something else, or even picturing different parts of the body, there is no need to comment on this. Just very gently become aware of where you feel the sensations of breathing in the body. That is all you have to do. Allow, and return attention to the body.

It can be very helpful to have an aid to keep you on task. Breath counting is a good way to do this. We still attend closely to the sensations of breathing, and add in a count, generally on the out breath. We do this by counting silently to ourselves one (oooonnnnnne) for the full length of the out breath, while still being aware of the breath in the body. Then, we breathe in, aware of the breath, and count again (twwwwoooo) on the out breath. All the way up to four. Then go back to one. This is not really a counting exercise, but a way to keep anchored to the breathing, and to the experience of breathing.

It is important to remember that there is no special, or right, way to breathe. Big deep breaths are not any better than shallow breaths. The aim is to let the breathing happen by itself. Although breathing happens on its own, once we attend to things, we habitually try to control them. Part of this exercise is giving up control. Letting the breath happen. And following from that, letting the sensations happen, letting the attention rest with the movement of the breath, while still not letting our attention be dragged off with every passing sensation, urge, or thought.

That's it, and that really is plenty to work with. For years. We can also be mindful of other things, like the feeling of our feet on the floor, the sound of birds, or passing traffic, wind on the skin. Anything at all. However, awareness of breath is a good foundation, and with practice leads to a wider open awareness, which includes the activities of daily life. With surprisingly little practice, we can bring this awareness to our chosen sporting activity. Before we can be truly effectively mindful during activity, we need to develop the stability of our attention, and be open to experience with minimal activity. In some ways, it's like learning to drive. You don't have your first driving lesson in the middle of London during rush hour, or on the freeway in LA. That is not going to go well. Mindfulness of breath is also like base training. It is not something you move on from, and give up. It is always useful.

Further suggestions

It can be extremely useful to have some instruction and support in mindfulness training. It is very easy to divert off into funny ways of practising. Almost any instruction we are given on mindfulness practice somehow gets distorted, and we slip back into our 'ideas' or expectations about how to practice mindfulness. This is our experience as both students and as people who teach mindfulness.

Problems encountered in mindfulness practice.

1. **Concentrating too hard.** Attention is needed; however, the best approach is to take a relaxed, open, attentive attitude to your experience. Hard concentration is tiring, and tends to narrow our attention.

2. **Trying not to think.** A lot of people assume that being mindful, or meditating means not thinking. Good luck not thinking. We don't know anyone who can do this for a prolonged period. Also, thinking is incredibly useful, in the right context. For our mindfulness practice, the aim is to not get hooked, or snagged by your thoughts. Don't let them drag you into their little story. We do this by very, very gently returning to the bodily sensations associated with breathing. This type of exercise develops flexibility. It develops the ability to choose when to get wrapped up in thoughts and when to attend to something else of our choice.

3. **Blanking out experience.** This is a little like concentrating too hard. When we begin our mindfulness practice, noises and sensations from other parts of the body might fade into the background, but we are not trying to get rid of these things. We don't aim to limit our experience. Just to attend as consistently as possible to the sensations of breathing. If other things become included, without dragging you away, then that is fine. Thoughts do tend to be very sticky in that they suck us in extremely easily. Therefore, it is good to simply let them be as they are and attend to the body.

4. **Expecting, or wanting to feel good, relaxed or blissed out.** It is common for people to feel good when practicing mindfulness. Sometimes people get very relaxed and feel that something special has happened. The natural inclination is to try and repeat this experience, or to achieve an experience like something we have read about. Sorry, we don't always feel good, and things don't always feel wonderful. Mindfulness practice is about what is happening right now. Not about what you want to happen. You might be tired, sad, angry, or hungry. It doesn't matter.

Those are all good times to practice. We are developing the ability to simply allow things as they are – so eventually we can respond to things in an open and flexible manner, where we are not being driven by events or internal states.

5. **Worried about not doing it right.** Some people often wonder if they are 'doing it right'. It is common to feel discouraged because you seem to be having a lot of thoughts, feel uncomfortable, or don't feel relaxed or all zen-ed out. Don't worry. If you are trying, you are doing it right. If you are distracted and notice that, you are doing it right. If you are annoyed, and go back to the breath, you are doing it right.

6. **Not Practising.** One of the most common problems is simply not sitting down to practise. Most people find that mindfulness practice is not really that hard, but sitting down to start it is. It helps to make a regular time, and just do it. You don't need to feel like it. You don't have to be motivated. You don't have to enjoy it. Simply make it something you do, much like brushing your teeth.

> You must unlearn what you have learned.
> Do or do not. There is no try.
>
> **Jedi Master Yoda**

Summary

- In this chapter, we introduced the Three Pillars of an ACT approach to psychological flexibility and performance enhancement – being open, aware, and engaged.

- Your practice for the next week is to record at least two instances or situations a day (for five of seven days this week) where you try to notice your bodily sensations, thoughts, and actions. Most people have problems with the bodily sensations, but give it your best shot. You will get better with practice. The more instances you write down, the better.

- The other practice is mindfulness. Mindfulness of breath is the best foundational practice for this. As long as you have a body, and are breathing, you can practice! We suggest practising for a minimum of ten minutes a day.

- Some people do find mindfulness practice hard. They are not used to sitting quietly, and tend to have very active minds which they find troublesome. If you do really feel like ten minutes is too much for you, do five minutes. It is much better to do five minutes a day, five to seven days a week, than two hours one day on the weekend. The regularity of practice is important.

In the next chapter, we will look at what makes life worth living, and why improving our performance is important. You can move straight to that chapter but remember to do the practices we have suggested for a week. Give them a good trial for one week, and see what you discover.

Things to Practise

Practice Activities:

- Record reactions and bodily sensations
- Practise mindfulness

Chapter 3

VALUES

Ask an elite runner if they like running, or racing, and they will probably say yes. Ask them if it hurts, and they will look at you like you are a bit simple and say, 'Yes. Of course, it hurts. It hurts a lot'. Do athletes like learning new skills, and getting better at what they do? Yes. Do they enjoy doing the same basic movements over and over, and over again, and not getting it quite right? Sometimes (even though it can be incredibly frustrating). Indeed, the pursuit of sport can bring out lots of negative thoughts and emotions. Things like 'I will never get this', 'I am useless', 'This is pathetic'.

So why do they do it?

Because of their desire to win, to be better, to master something, even simply to master the fear of failure. But there is something else there, something intangible. Generally, we do it because we love it; pure and simple. It doesn't make sense in logical terms. Why put yourself through that pain? Why let other parts of your life suffer? Why not play games on the computer, go get a pizza and a drink, or just lie in bed in the morning? It is that intangible 'I love it just because I do' aspect that is a key component of ACT. The part we call Values. Values here simply mean those parts of life we place value on; the parts which are valuable to us.

It is common to use negative self-talk, frustration, and even anger to drive performance. For many athletes, this can be the default position when wanting to push themselves and achieve. One of the problems with this strategy is that we get so wrapped up in our thoughts, and the associated negative emotions that go with them, that (over time) this feels normal. It can become our main, if not our only, strategy for motivation. So, we use the feeling that 'I am useless' to drive practice. We use pride, 'I can't let her beat me!' We use the internal command 'I have to train', and the fear of failure, of embarrassment, of letting others down, of being 'a loser' as a way to push ourselves and achieve. In psychology, this is called aversive control. It is considered a form of 'punishment' because behaviour is being driven by wanting to avoid something negative, or unpleasant. With these types of motivators, we are using an escape/avoidance strategy. We are trying to avoid something bad rather than going after something we want; something good.

Behaviour that is driven by seeking out something positive – going after something we want – on the other hand, is under appetitive control. This is similar to 'appetite' and reflects behaviour driven by desire rather than avoidance. When behaviour is under appetitive control, it is reward-focused and feels more positive. With aversive control, by comparison, people are always looking – consciously or unconsciously – for a way to escape the situation. While this can be successful, it ultimately involves wasted energy. It creates frustration, tension, self-doubt, fear, and of course 'choking'. It is no surprise that aversive control is less effective than appetitive control.

If we are clear about our values, and what is important to us, we can use this knowledge to create meaningful, satisfying goals and motivators. We can work more consciously towards something positive in what we do, rather than being driven by negatives. You can think of it as the difference between being whipped (literally) out to practice, as opposed to joyfully going out to see what it will be like today.

To illustrate the difference between aversive and appetitive control, think about what it would be like for someone picked randomly off the street being forced to lift heavy weights, do wind sprints, and burpees. It would be like torture (in fact, it reminds us a little of third form gym class). Compare that to the experience of those who do exactly the same things, but who choose to do it and see it as a positive. This may seem like an extreme example, but if you have spent much time training, you have probably felt pain and felt forced – by yourself or others – into activities you didn't like, and which you resented. By focusing more on values, we don't try to get rid of the negatives, or ignore them, we simply become more aware of what is really important to us. Although we might not always enjoy what we do, we do find it meaningful.

Before we describe how to use 'values' in practice, we need to know what values are from an ACT point of view. More importantly, you need to be clear what your values are. What is it that is really meaningful to you? This is not a one-size-fits-all practice.

What Are Values?

We have already started to examine how we get 'fused' with our thoughts. How our automatic reactions and expectations can blind us to other possibilities, and other ways of acting. Caught up in this 'fusion', along with the demands of everyday living, and in responding automatically, we can often lose sight of what is important to us; the things that make life worthwhile. In the realm of any creative, challenging, or high-performance activity, we can lose sight of why we are doing it in the first place. This happens as we naturally tend to focus on more immediate demands and goals rather than what led us to set those goals in the first place. What we refer to as values, are those aspects of life that have a special resonance, or importance to us, and which ideally drive our behaviour. Such as our engagement in certain sports.

It is important to be clear on what we mean by values. They are not to be confused with values in the sense of morals, or what we think of as right or wrong. For our purposes, values simply mean those things that we appraise highly. They have meaning for us for some reason. For some people, being a good parent is a value. It is important to them. Others really enjoy gardening or going for a run, even though this is technically work. It takes effort, and it is not always pleasurable, or easy. It is, in a way, special. It not only makes them feel good, it has some meaning that is hard to define.

The trouble is, we often confuse a goal (running a marathon, lifting a target weight, or cutting the hedges) with the value itself. Enjoying the feeling of being fit, the act of running, spending time in nature, being creative or productive – they are values. Confusing the goal with the value, or valued activity, means that sometimes, even though we are doing things in line with our values, we are dissatisfied. That is because all our focus is on a goal rather than on the value our activity reflects or 'is in the service of'. Also, most of the time, a specific goal is not met while we are trying to achieve it. We may fail to see that we can be feeding our values, keeping them alive, by going for a walk, a short run, or having a cup of coffee in the garden. Or, by taking our argumentative children to school, we can be living our values even though things prove uncomfortable. The argument in our head, if we bother to pay attention to it, can often go something like: 'This isn't good enough, it would be better if...', and other ideas about how things would be better 'if only'. In this example, there are two things going on: fusion with thoughts, and a lack of attention to values.

Values and Goals

There is nothing wrong with goals. Goals are fine. Having clearly defined and progressive goals helps us to achieve. They help to give a structure and a pattern to our practice. The downside is that an over-focus on goals, without an active awareness of values, can lead to a persistent sense of dissatisfaction. When the goal is met, we feel good for a while, then we need to find another goal.

Another difficulty with only focusing on goals is what has been termed destructive goal pursuit. Christopher Kayes has described this in his discussions of the Mount Everest Disaster, when 12 climbers died on Everest in 1996 with eight dying in one day. The popularity of climbing Everest, and in guided climbs, has grown greatly in recent years and the number of climbers attempting to summit 'Chomolungma' has increased significantly.

Due to the dangerousness of the mountain, and the changing weather conditions, it is important to begin your descent of Everest in time to avoid navigating the most treacherous areas in the dark. What Kayes noticed, during a trip to the Himalayas, was that a number of climbers died over the course of one day, due to not beginning their return in time, and there was a very specific reason they did this. The final hundred metres or so to the summit of Mount Everest is limited to a narrow track. This means climbers have to move in a single file in this area. There were so many climbers returning that those waiting to get to the summit had queued up waiting. It was only 100 metres after all. They had nearly reached their goal. Many climbers, including their guides, dangerously delayed their descent hoping they would find time to make it to the summit. As a result, eight people died. Their focus on the short-term goal blinded them to the bigger picture.

Kayes has gone on to identify how narrow goal attainment in other areas can lead not only to a failure to be truly productive, but to various disasters or failures related to cutting corners, by not taking sufficient safety precautions, and poor preparation. Any athlete who has ever suffered an injury due to overtraining, or doing 'something stupid', can probably understand the concept of destructive goal attainment quite well!

When applying ACT to the area of performance, we want to avoid an excessively narrow focus on goals. We want to be aware of the big picture, and what makes our activity truly nourishing and fulfilling. The values are the priority; the goal is a marker along the way on the bigger journey.

Values, as described in ACT, have certain characteristics. They are typically vague. They can never be fully achieved. They are like a general direction we take in life, not a specific destination. Living according to your values is typically described as like going west. You can go from where you live to the town west of you. Then to the town west of that. You can travel west to the coast, and across the ocean. Going west across the next continent you come to, and across another ocean. You can keep going west, forever. Just like we can always be a better parent, and can continue to do things to be healthy, or creative, or to develop a skill. The upside of that is that any little thing we do towards our values is positive; we are winning. When we do something in line with our values, at that point we are fully living them; just like every little step towards west is going in the right direction.

Some people will be familiar with SMART goals, a way to identify and structure goals in order to make them more attainable. Values are the opposite of SMART goals. They are not:

- **S**pecific
- **M**easurable
- **A**chievable
- **R**ealistic
- **T**ime-framed

Let's take an example. Getting a house is a goal. It is achievable. Values aren't achievable, so we need to look a little deeper. Why do you want a house? There could be a lot of reasons. If it is so you can have a nice place to relax and do your own thing, have a nice garden, or kick back and play the guitar, that is fine. That is what is important to you. But if you spend all your time at work paying for the house, you can lose sight of why you wanted it in the first place. In the same way, training can become a drag. You have to go; you are tired, you don't feel like it, it takes up too much time. We tend to lose sight of the fact that, on some basic level, we not only enjoy it but that it reflects something important in our lives.

People can have lots of different ideas about what values are. To be clear, when we talk about values in this book, we are talking about principles or qualities that guide us in living the life we truly want to live. Your values are what make your life worth living. Because values are quite vague, it can be useful to have a good understanding of what they are, and what they are not.

Values are guideposts. Values are not goals, and they cannot be achieved. For example, getting married is a goal. Being loving and caring in relationships is a value. Values are a direction (e.g., West), and goals are a destination (e.g., Los Angeles, or Perth). You can keep going west your whole life, but once you reach Los Angeles, you've accomplished your goal. Making a team, winning a competition, or setting a personal best are all fine goals. They are not the values that lie behind those goals.

Values are expressed as behaviours. They serve as guides to what you do. They aren't things you have. Being loving is something you do, while being loved is something you have. We can't control whether other people love us. But we can control how we behave, and that then influences other people's behaviour. Values aren't emotions either. Wanting to be happy is a goal, and most likely a futile one as we can't stay happy all the time. Likewise, being a winner is a goal; being a runner is a value.

Values are personal. Nobody can tell you what you should, or shouldn't, value – it's about what makes your life meaningful, or worth living; not what your family, coach, boss or friends think will make your life worth living!

Discovering Values

Exercise One – The Funeral

This is an exercise in imagination. For this exercise, we would like you to read through the brief instructions first, then settle back and go through the process we describe.

Before we begin the exercise, sit back, close your eyes, and relax a little. Take a couple of deep breaths and when you breathe out, let your back relax, let your shoulders drop, and loosen your jaw. Let this happen over the course of several breaths. Then, let your breathing come naturally without trying to control it.

When you have relaxed, imagine a scene where – through some miracle – you are at your own funeral. What we want you to do is to pick three, maybe four, people to get up and talk about the kind of person you were in your life. They can be living people, dead people, or even those not born yet. Whoever pops into your head is good. If someone comes up and you think 'no, not them', they would probably be a good person to pick.

Now, because this is an exercise in imagination, we don't want people to say the types of things you would necessarily expect them to say, or to use the types of words they would normally use. For this exercise, it is important that these people say how you, in your deepest heart, would like them to have seen you. It is important that this is what you want, not what others expect or desire. In this exercise we want them to describe the type of person you wish you were. It's very important to remember that this is not based on reality. It's not based on the way you have been, what you have done, or how you think people see you. It's based on how you would like to be. Because it is important that you are honest with yourself, we are not going to ask you to write this exercise down, take notes, or share it with anyone. When we give workshops with this material, we make this point very clearly.

This exercise can help you to answer this question. How do you want to have lived your life, and how would that be reflected in what is seen by these people who, for better or worse, are/were important in your life?

Typically, this is not an easy exercise or a quick one. If you fly through this exercise in a minute or two, we suggest you go back, take your time, and do it again.

Once you've completed this exercise, think back over the things people have said and see if you can identify any common themes. These themes might give you an insight into some of the core values that you hold.

Exercise Two – The Tombstone Exercise

Whilst thinking of the things people said about you in the Funeral Exercise, and any themes you noticed, draw a tombstone on a piece of paper and in a few words write down the type of person you would like to be remembered as. Not something formal like 'Here Lies Johnny Porter, he will be missed.' Just a few simple words, for example. . .

. . . something that expresses the values and themes you noticed.

While we feel these exercises are very important in helping to identify values, they really are preliminary exercises. Something to get us in touch with what's important to us. Now, we can begin to become more specific about what our values are, and how we can translate them into our lives.

Exercise Three – Values Identification

Next are some domains or areas of life where people commonly find value. These are not the only types of values that there are, so we have left some spaces on the chart for you to add your own. For example, creativity is a value that comes up quite often which people add to the list. Another is being in nature. You can see from these examples that the values are quite broad, and we want you to think generally about what is important to you. We will get more specific later on.

In this exercise, we would like you to rate the importance (to you) of different common areas of life. Not what is expected of you, not what society says, not what your family want, and not what your friends think.

For example, work is often thought of as being important, but if you only work so you afford to ski, it is not really a value. It is simply a means to an end. It's not that important as a value. Also, if you are a parent, then a general societal expectation is that being a parent should be of high importance. The reality is that, at different stages in our lives, different things take priority; maybe parenting is not that important at the moment. On the other hand, many people don't have children, but the function of parenting – caring for others, guiding them, and helping them – is very important.

While people often have similar values, they can express themselves very differently. Spirituality, for instance, can be going to church every week for some people, and for others it is expressed as walking on the beach. Take your time and think broadly about these different areas and rate the importance of them for you.

This isn't a graded exercise where one value has to be more important than another. You can have three tens, and four zeros; that is fine. Please put an X over the number that best expresses the importance of each value to you. Exactly as in the Funeral Exercise, these ratings have nothing at all to do with your behaviour, with what you do; they are all about how important a value is to you.

Value	Low Importance___High Importance
Family	0 1 2 3 4 5 6 7 8 9 10
Recreation	0 1 2 3 4 5 6 7 8 9 10
Work	0 1 2 3 4 5 6 7 8 9 10
Friends	0 1 2 3 4 5 6 7 8 9 10
Intimate Relationships	0 1 2 3 4 5 6 7 8 9 10
Self-care	0 1 2 3 4 5 6 7 8 9 10
Education	0 1 2 3 4 5 6 7 8 9 10
Spirituality	0 1 2 3 4 5 6 7 8 9 10
Community	0 1 2 3 4 5 6 7 8 9 10
[Other]	0 1 2 3 4 5 6 7 8 9 10
[Other]	0 1 2 3 4 5 6 7 8 9 10
[Other]	0 1 2 3 4 5 6 7 8 9 10

Once you have rated the aspects of life that are important to you – that you value – look at the four highest. Write them down on a sheet of paper, and think about what your life would be like if you were living in line with these values. What would you be doing?

Some examples people have come up with have been: spending time with family, joining a community group, taking better care of themselves by getting more sleep. Things like that. These are pretty normal things. You don't have to think of some grand activity, simply a few things that would put you more in line with your values. Write down some of the things you would do on a regular basis that would reflect your values in different areas.

Once you have done that, think about living that life. What would it feel like? Would it be good? Or satisfying?

Now, rate how consistent you have been in living, according to your values, over the past two weeks. Using the same scale, draw a circle around the number that best represents how consistent you have been. Say you gave self-care a nine in importance, but in the last few weeks you have been really poor at living in line with this value. In that case, you would rate consistency much lower than nine. If you were right where you wanted to be, then you would circle the nine. On the other hand, if work was a four in importance and you have been doing 60-hour weeks, then you might give work a ten on consistency and this represents that it was way out of line with importance. It was overrepresented in what you did.

If you are like most people, you probably felt a bit of a sinking feeling when noticing the differences between your values and your behaviour. This is normal. No one has the perfect life, and we are certainly not suggesting that anyone could, or should, allocate specific amounts of time to different activities each and every day – forever – in order to have the mythical 'balanced' lifestyle. Life doesn't work like that.

Sometimes we prioritise certain interests, and sometimes others. People often devote a lot of time to particular interests for a while, then get more involved in other things and move back and forth between their passions. In other words, people seem to be happier, and feel more fulfilled, when they are interested, engaged, and doing what has meaning for them. Then, due to circumstance, or a slight change in interests, they become more involved in other things; they don't give up the other activity, it just becomes less of a focus for a while.

Sport is one area where this shift in focus is common. When training for a specific event, or during the 'season' of your sport, more time is required, and other things take a back seat. That is just the nature of being devoted to certain interests. What is imperative is that we can find ways to keep the other areas of our lives active, even in a small way. They provide sustenance, satisfaction, and the energy to devote effort to our other endeavours.

The ratings you have made are just a snapshot in time. Maybe the last two weeks have been unusual for you, but have a look at your differences between importance and consistency. If you notice some areas where things you value have been neglected, and this has been a long-term trend, take note. Write them down. These are areas that you can target. It is possible to move consistently towards your values with only small changes.

Living Your Values

Now we want to look at ways of living your values.

We want to look at how to find small changes that 'feed', or keep alive, those things that are meaningful to you, but which can often be put to one side while we do things that are 'more important'.

John Lennon once said, 'Life is what happens when you are busy making other plans.' What we want to do is find ways that whilst 'life happens' we are fully living it, rather than just letting it happen to us. That means being more open, aware, engaged, and flexible.

One way to be more fully engaged in the things we do, is by being more mindful and aware. The mindfulness exercise we suggested in the previous chapter focuses on this. Another way is to be consciously aware of what is important, meaningful, or sustaining for us, and to incorporate this into what we do. Making it part of our behaviour. We will look at broad, general values first, and then go on to identify, and work with, more sport-specific related values.

We have looked at your values, and asked what type of things you would be doing if you were living your life in a way that reflected what was most important to you. When asked this question, people often mention things like: spend more time with family, exercise, or train more, contact friends, spend more time in creative pursuits, and (even) do more to clean up around the house. These seem like ordinary, even mundane things and, in a way, they are. They also reflect important aspects of people's lives like: family, friends, self-care, the desire to move, being active, and striving. There are many ways to move toward, or to 'feed', these values. We don't have to visit friends and family if other priorities make this difficult, or impossible. We can phone, or text, or send an e-mail. Remember, anything that supports the broad value is supporting a valued, worthwhile life.

One of the authors remembers a period, as a young man, when he felt it wasn't worth training unless he could do two-hour sessions. Not training at the intensity he was used to felt like going backwards, retreating from his goals. Returning to University, and having a young child, made it difficult to regularly put aside this amount of time to train. It was very frustrating to limit training, and it ultimately led to increased intensity, overtraining, and injuries when he was able to train. A lot of unnecessary frustration, dissatisfaction, and suffering could have been avoided by focusing more on valued activities such as short sessions at a reasonable intensity and load (as opposed to focusing on goals and expectations).

We suggest a five-step plan as a way to begin to develop living a valued life.

> **Exercise Four — Living your values**
>
> 1. List your three top priority values.
>
> 2. Identify five small behaviours that support, or are in line with, those values.
>
> 3. Schedule at least one per day, to do in the next week. Preferably, try to do something in line with feeding different values when possible.
>
> 4. Notice how you feel when you engage in these activities and afterwards. Use the recording sheet we introduced in the last chapter to help notice and record your reactions to consciously engaging in small

valued activities. Remember, they don't have to be fun, just meaningful.

5. Do steps 3 to 5 again. And again, and again, for at least five days. Unrealistic goals aren't helpful, and no one is perfect. If you aim for five days, you might get three. Aim for seven days and take five as a win – with room for improvement.

1. **Identifying values to work on.**
   This should be easy. Just look at the values you identified in Exercise Three, and either pick the top three values or, if your life is going well in some of those areas, pick a value that is important to you, but which has been neglected for some time. That is, where your actions have not reflected the importance or value you place on that aspect of your life.

2. **Find behaviours that are consistent with, or which foster, that value.**
   Sometimes, appropriate behaviours can seem difficult. That is because we often focus on goals, or on specific activities. Imagine that

you want to go for a run, but for some reason (injury, time, or other unavoidable demands) you can't. As a result, you feel frustration. Your psychology advisor suggests you go for a walk instead. That, of course, feels completely ridiculous. In fact, stupid.

For a whole host of reasons. But what is your value? Is running a value? Or is being active, being outdoors, and being healthy the value? Running this week is a goal; being active, or healthy, is a value. How can we feed these values? Going for a walk is one way. So is swimming, doing some simple stretching, or a few push-ups. There are lots of ways to feed a value. All we have to do is think broadly about what is consistent with our values. Remember, in general, it is not the activity that is important; it is the value that it supports or gives life to. Running is an expression of being healthy, or of being physically fit. So is walking, stretching, and even getting enough sleep. Values can be expressed in multiple ways.

Now, going for a ten-minute walk (as opposed to a half-hour run) might seem pointless in terms of training, and in meeting goals. There can be resistance to identifying, and engaging in, these small behaviours as we feel they are 'not good enough'. We tend to get caught up in thoughts about how things 'should' be, and about what we 'want', or what we expect. This type of resistance can be a barrier not only to identifying a range of values, and values-consistent behaviours, but to engaging in them later on. We will talk about this more when discussing barriers to action.

3. **Engage in at least one small values-driven behaviour a day.**
Make these activities small. Especially at first. When we start working with values-driven behaviour, the main aim is to be aware of what our values are, the different ways they can be expressed, and to start to do this consciously, with awareness. You will be much more successful if you start to engage in small values-driven behaviours consistently on a regular basis. Of course, very few people follow this advice; at least at first. Taking on tasks that are too big, or too ambitious, usually leads to long-term failure. If you don't manage

to do your planned valued behaviours, don't beat yourself up. Start again; and start with something small.

4. **Notice how you feel after you complete values-consistent behaviour.**
   This is important. As we have said previously, valued behaviour isn't always fun at the time. It is meaningful, and it helps make a life worth living. Check in with how you feel when doing the values-driven activity, and how you feel afterwards; even the next day. Make use of the recording sheet we introduced in the previous chapter to make these insights more concrete by writing them down.

5. **Do steps 3 to 5 again.**
   A beautiful (and perhaps slightly unfortunate) fact of life is that just because you might have done something really well once, you are not done. You are not living in the past; you are living right now. What are you going to do today? How is your life going to be the life you want today? This means going through the whole process again. Then the next day, and

the day after that, and the day after that. This is the nature of commitment.

Of course, for the purposes of this book, what we are doing here is: training your ability to notice valued activities, noticing positive (or negative) feedback from these activities, and practising a desired class of behaviour (valued activities) on a regular basis. As in all training, this requires repetition. The more you consciously practise, especially with small activities, the more your skill in this area will develop. This will serve you well when you focus on valued behaviour in specific relation to your sporting activity.

Values in Sport

We will approach this in the same way that we looked at values in general. Just with more of an emphasis on your sporting life.

The 80th Birthday Exercise

This is just like the Funeral Exercise. Do it the same way. The only difference is that you imagine you are at your 80th birthday party, and the people there are talking about the type of person you were in your sporting life. Again, this is not necessarily related to how you have behaved; it is all about how you would like to have acted, how you would have behaved if you lived in line with your values.

Just as in the Funeral Exercise, relax a little, and when you are ready, pick three, or four people to get up and talk about the kind of person you were when you took part in sports. What you were like. They might talk about what kind of competitor you were. Or, what kind of friend you were. Remember that they are going to describe your ideal. They are going to put into words how you wish you were. These can be people living or dead, or even people not born yet. Whoever pops into your head is good. Again, if someone comes up and you think 'no, not them', they would probably be a good person to pick. Take your time with this exercise.

Remember that when we ask how you want others to see you, it is not so much about how we want to be seen, but how we want to be. It is not about image, but how we behave. As social creatures, we tend to view ourselves through the eyes of others. They are important to us. In this exercise, as in the Funeral Exercise, the aim is to identify the type of person you want to be.

Once you have finished, see if you can identify any themes amongst what people said. If so, write the themes down.

This is an important exercise in getting in touch with what is important to us in how we behave in the context of our sporting life. Now, it is time to be much more specific about what kind of player, or sports person you want to be. Not what others think you should be.

Exercise Five – Values in the context of sport

Think about being at the end of your athletic career, and then answer the following questions. Be sure to write your answers down. Remember, this is how you would ideally like to be, not necessarily how you are, or how you usually act. It is also not about measures of performance in the sense of goals scored, times run, or outs per over. It is about actions that reflect your values.

1. What kind of person would you like to be seen as by teammates, training partners, and coaches?

2. How would you like your children to see you? If you don't have children, imagine you do; or how you would like younger players/athletes to see you?

3. What kind of sportsperson would you like to be, for your family?

4. What kind of person would you like your opponents to see you as?

5. What qualities would you like to see in your behaviour as a sports person, or athlete? How do you want to be?

Now, considering your answers to the five questions above; if you were living in line with your values, what would that look like? What would you be doing? In the context of your sport, training, competition, and your interactions with others, what actions would demonstrate your values? Be specific. For each of the questions – one to five – write down what values-driven actions would look like for you. Think carefully about this. These don't have to be grand behaviours. It is best to focus on simple, ordinary actions.

Everyone's responses to this will be different. There are no right or wrong answers here. An example for number one might be in line with broad values of doing the best for the team, and supporting others in providing their best efforts.

1. 'I wouldn't slack off as much in training or pull faces when the coach asks us to do something hard'. Equally, a response could be, 'I would speak up when I think the coach is wrong, or he is picking on someone', or simply 'I will show up for the weekly run more often'.

The aim here is to think broadly about not only your values as ideas, but also about your behaviour. The things you do, both large and small, that are more in line with how you want to be as a person, and as an athlete.

Do this for all five of the questions before you read any further.

Exercise Six – the Bull's Eye

This exercise is adapted from the Bull's Eye developed by Swedish Psychologist Tobias Lundgren. Here, we will look at how consistent you have been in living in line with your values. You can think of this diagram as a dart board. The board is divided into four quarters, one for different types of relationships, and one for values not captured in the other quadrants. Thinking about the past two weeks, how consistent have you been in living your values? Place an **X** in the ring that best represents your overall values-driven behaviour over the last two weeks. If the X is in the centre of the bull's eye, your actions were as close as you can get to being consistent with your values. That doesn't mean you were always successful in meeting your goals, but that your overall actions were in line with what you value.

As the rings move further away from the centre, they represent less value-driven behaviour. As an illustration, Wayne values being healthy; he enjoys running, it is his main sport, and he hasn't gone for a run for the past two weeks. He hasn't done any other exercise either. There can be legitimate reasons for this – like illness or injury – but he was inconsistent with this value. In this case, he would place an **X** in one of the outer rings.

For each of the four quadrants – Family /children, Teammates, etc., place an X on the dartboard to denote how you are living your life before moving on to the next part of the exercise.

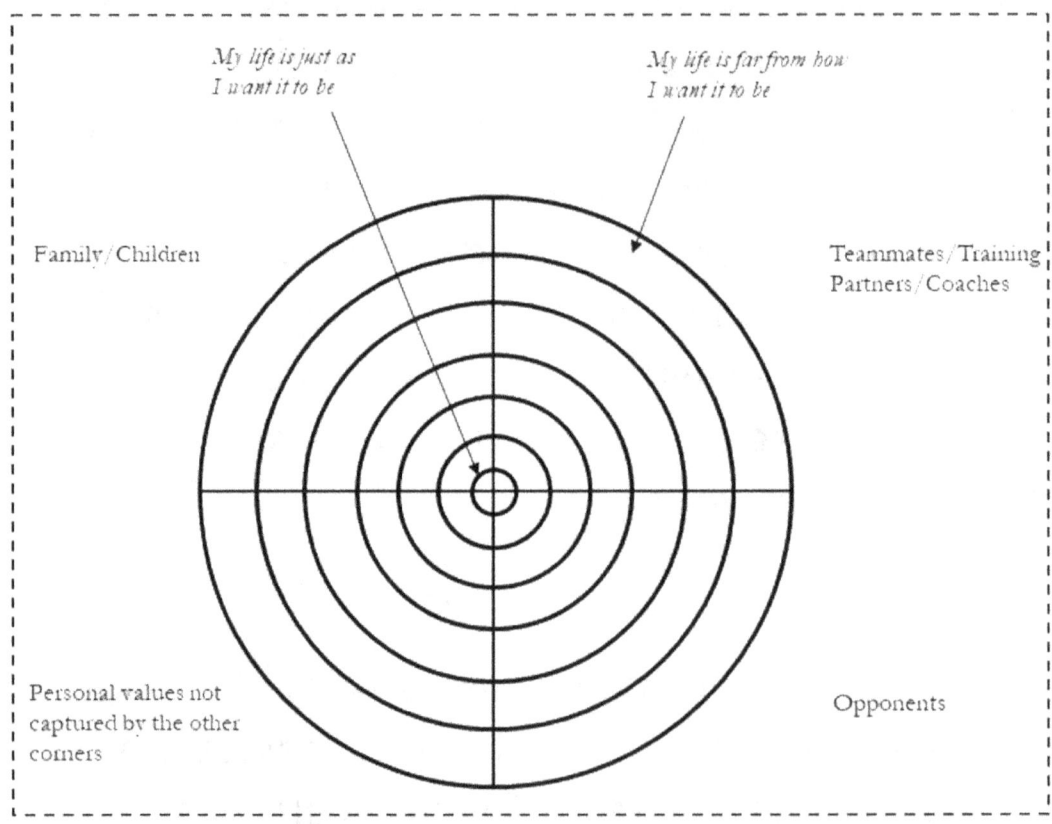

Looking at the Xs you placed on the Bull's Eye, consider how successful you have been in living your values. If you are not where you want to be, what has stopped you? What gets in the way? Describe, in writing, what the barriers are to you hitting the bull's eye in each quadrant. It can be external circumstances or just a lack of action on your part. It doesn't matter, write it down. In some cases, the obstacle might be the same for more than one area (that is fine). Do think carefully though.

Now, estimate how much each of those obstacles have stopped you from living your life in a way that is in keeping with your values. On a piece of paper, underneath each obstacle, write out the numbers one to seven. One means 'doesn't stop me at all', and seven means 'stops me completely'. Circle the number that best describes how powerful the obstacle has been in your life recently.

Doesn't stop me at all						Stops me completely
1	2	3	4	5	6	7

A Plan of Action

In Exercise five, you made a list of things you would be doing in your sporting activity if you were living in line with your values. List those under the four quadrants from the Bull's Eye. That is, values-related behaviours in relation to:

- Teammates, training partners, and coaches
- Family
- Opponents or other competitors
- Other Personal Values

Think of as many behaviours as you can. The more, the better.

In Exercise Four, we looked at values in general. Some of those values are probably also reflected in the more specific sports-related values you identified. The sports-related behaviours may be different though, as they apply to more specific situations. As in Exercise Four, you have now identified behaviours that support or reflect your sports-related values. To put these into practice...

1. Schedule in at least one values-based action a day, during the next week.

2. Notice how you feel when you engage in these activities and afterwards. Use the recording sheet we introduced in the last chapter to help notice and record your reaction to consciously engaging in small valued activities.

3. Do this every day for at least five days.

Also, notice the things that get in the way of you putting your valued actions into practice. Write these down on your record sheet. We will be looking at ways of dealing with barriers or obstacles as we go on.

Summary

- In this chapter, we looked at what is meaningful in life, and what is fundamentally important to you about your sporting activity. In other words, we identified what makes the effort of doing the exercises in this book worthwhile.

- We also began to look at what actions you can take to consistently move towards your ideals, and what gets in the way.

- If you have completed the exercises in this chapter, you will have a plan of action to start living more in line with your values.

In the next chapter, we will look more closely at dealing with specific barriers to performance. In doing this, we will expand on the mindfulness practice introduced in the previous chapter and develop those skills to deal with problems as they arise in the midst of action. We will also introduce two other exercises that we continue to develop in remaining chapters as tools for fostering openness, awareness, and engagement.

Chapter 4

PASSENGERS (MONSTERS) ON THE BUS

In the last chapter, we talked about why you choose to play your sport. We explored the underlying values that inform how you would like to live and which way you are heading. The next step is to translate these values into specific actions that will take you in that direction.

As an athlete, everyone faces external difficulties: finding time to train, getting appropriate training advice, or joining a team that is a good fit for you, and what you want. There are other challenges, though, that can be much harder. Challenges that can't be overcome by normal problem-solving or planning. These are your internal barriers. The barriers we are talking about here are the habits of thinking, and reacting emotionally, that block or stifle potential. We refer to them as 'passengers (or monsters) on the bus'. They can be things like self-doubt, being overly critical of ourselves, anxiety, and fear of failure.

If you pay attention to these passengers, or as most of us do – work hard to avoid noticing them at all – it causes problems.

The 'passengers' you carry with you are the subject of the following chapters. In this chapter, we will explain how you can get to know your own personal passengers.

The Journey

One way to think about how these passengers can impact upon us, is to imagine you are driving towards living the life you want; moving towards living in line with your values.

The road is bumpy at times, there are delays, but you can handle that.

VALUES

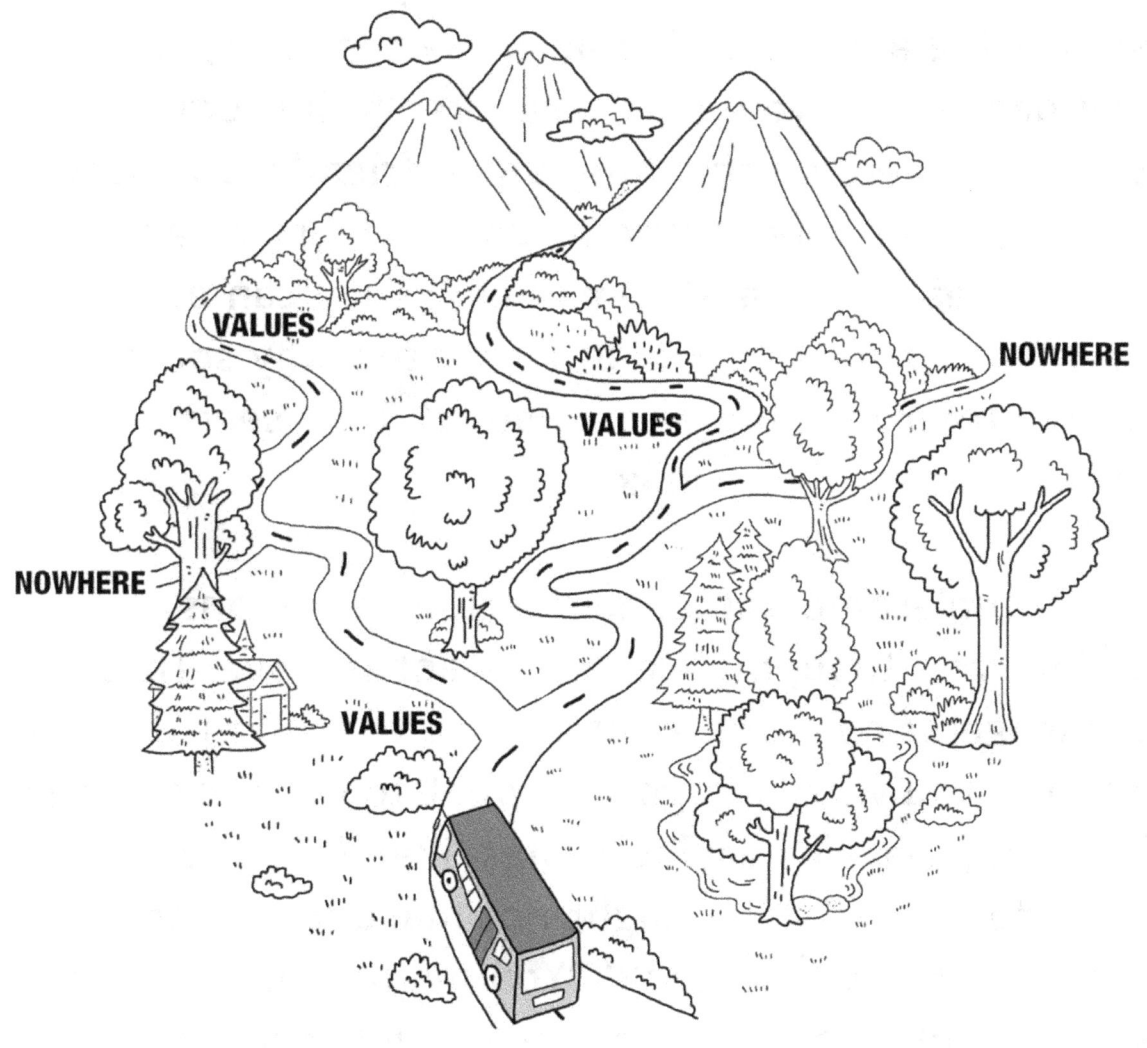

The thing is, you are not alone on your bus. Like everyone else, you carry your history with you. You have learned various things over your life: ways of thinking, habits, and ways of reacting. We all carry a rich and varied learning history with us. That includes different ways of being or acting in different situations. As a result, when you move towards your values, you are not driving a sports car. You are driving a bus carrying all these thoughts, fears, and habits with you as passengers. While some of the passengers on this bus can be friendly and very helpful, others are pretty unruly. They are often rude, threatening, and demanding. They can even be frightening. That is another reason why some people refer to them as 'monsters'. They seem big, insurmountable, and in control.

The troublesome passengers include emotions, beliefs, and thoughts we don't want to have. These passengers/monsters want to take control of the bus and tell you where to go and what to do. They do this in sneaky ways by saying things like, 'This is too hard now, do it later', 'You might not make it, and then everyone knows you can't', 'You might find out that you are not as good as you think, and then what?'

Such internal comments can make you feel hopeless, anxious, and weary.

Following these directions can be virtually automatic. It seems to keep the peace – it keeps the passengers fairly quiet – but it diverts us from heading in the directions of our values, and thus living the life we want.

In order to keep moving in the direction you want, you will have to learn to deal with these internal struggles. As you do so, you will change and learn as a person along the way. This is not always going to be like a walk on the beach with an ice cream in hand. Rather, it will be a trip that will have challenges and adventures... if you let it.

As we learned from the previous exercises on mindfulness, you are not simply your emotions or your thoughts. These are things you 'have' rather than things you 'are'. This realisation is one of the main benefits of repeated mindfulness practice. It helps us to defuse from our thoughts. Rather than believing a thought and feeling it to be 100% true ('I am completely useless'), we realize that this is just one of many thoughts and feelings ('I really made a mess of that this time. I wonder what is for tea?'). The thought and the feeling associated with it is not 'me'. This realisation doesn't mean the thought or feeling isn't unpleasant. What it does do, however, is make it easier for us not to hang on to it and make a story out of it. A story that keeps the negative feeling going for longer.

Emotional/thinking reactions are often strongly ingrained, and difficult to deal with. Recognising them is only the first step. There are three main ways people typically deal with these reactions, these monsters, or passengers, that want to hijack the bus. We are going to run through them, so you can see which one is most familiar to you.

This next exercise has been called both 'Monsters on the Bus' and 'Passengers on the Bus'; we like the term monsters as it conveys the sense of how difficult it can be to deal with some of these ingrained patterns of reacting. However, many of these barriers to performance, and ways of moving away from living the life we want, are quite subtle. In many cases, the term 'passenger' seems more appropriate. In the text, we will refer to the thoughts and fears we want to avoid, as both passengers and monsters.

Monsters on the Bus

To make this more relevant to your situation, it is important to think back to your values. Look at what you wrote down. What were your main values both in life and in relation to your participation in sport? Think about them again and imagine what your life would be like if you were living in a way consistent with your values. What would you be doing? What would a typical day look like? A typical week? Who would you be seeing? How much time would you devote to different activities? Take your time and think it through, imagining a value-driven life. Write it down, or say it out loud.

If you are describing the life you want, it probably sounds pretty good. Now imagine you are driving the bus. You are heading in the direction of your values, towards that life you want. If you are sitting down, you might want to look around and find an actual physical direction that will represent the direction of your values; where you want to go. It could be towards a window, or a door, or towards an object in the room. Find something to represent the direction you want to go in. Imagine you are heading in that direction. You are moving towards your values; then your passengers show up (use the word monster if that fits better for you). These can be thoughts, but they are often feelings or general beliefs. You will have a good idea of what they are, from your own experience, and from having made records of the type of things you struggle with earlier on. Common passengers that people bring up are:

- 'I don't feel like training today.'
- 'I will fail.' / 'I am a failure.'
- 'I'm not good enough.'
- 'No one likes me.'
- 'I look stupid.'
- 'People will laugh at me.' or 'People are laughing at me.'
- 'Something terrible will happen.'
- 'It's no use trying.'
- 'It's useless.'
- 'I will always be alone.'
- 'I can't trust them.'

- 'I'm fat.'
- 'I am useless.'
- 'I am pathetic.'

The reason we often refer to these statements as monsters is because they can create very strong emotions. Emotions we want to avoid. We all have different beliefs, fears, and worries that serve as triggers for us. They bite deeper. They feel more real than most of the things that go through our heads. Other thoughts and ideas just don't have the same impact. The thing is that our triggers – our difficult passengers – get a reaction from us. So how do people typically try to cope with these passengers?

Exercise One – Avoid

This is possibly the most common reaction. We don't want to feel the emotion, so we shy away from situations where it comes up. This can be from complete avoidance of a situation, such as 'I am not going to compete today because I don't want to fail or look stupid' to moving slightly away from a head-on confrontation with the trigger. This could be by not quite giving our best in a competition; that way, we know we didn't really try and, therefore, we didn't really fail. These small aspects of avoidance come up in training, and in personal practice, all the time; avoiding practising what we are not good at, not giving full effort, even not thinking about certain things. Swearing and showing anger over errors are also ways of trying to avoid feeling bad – replacing one emotion with another.

You can demonstrate the effect of this, yourself. Stand, or sit, facing the direction that represents your values and think of, at least three, of your monsters. These are three of the thoughts/beliefs you want to avoid. Deal with one passenger at a time. Say (out loud) the type of thoughts that this passenger brings up. If one of your passengers is 'I'm not good enough', a whole range of thoughts can come up in association with this. As you say these thoughts in your normal voice, take your time and pay attention to your body. See if you feel some of the negative feelings that these comments trigger. Then, while staying in the same spot, turn facing to the right. This signifies moving slightly away from the negative feelings. Not running away, but gently avoiding. Each time you give words to one of your passengers, turn slightly to the right. Do this for at least three of the monsters on your bus. Do no more than four different monsters, at most.

When you have done this, notice which direction you are facing. Is it towards your values? How does facing this way feel? Did doing this exercise – moving aside from your values, avoiding the feelings – feel familiar? Write down your answers to these questions.

Exercise Two – Argue

Another way of dealing with these troublesome passengers is to argue with them. Just as in the last example, sit or stand facing in a direction that represents where your values lie. Call to mind what life would be like if you were living fully in line with those values. Using the same 'passengers' as before, say the thoughts that go with that feeling / thought out loud.

When you do this, try to connect with the feeling you get when you say the words, or what it has felt like in the past when this passenger was a real problem. Then, argue with them. Basically, talk to yourself, saying what the passenger thinks, and then disagreeing. Tell them they are wrong. Tell them why they are wrong. If you can't think of an argument, just contradict what the passenger or monster brings up. Let them argue with you, giving their view. Then answer back. Taking both parts like this can be difficult, so take your time and try to make a good argument.

When one of the authors was at school, he often rode the school bus. There were occasions when the bus driver, who was usually very friendly, would stop the bus, turn around and shout at all of the disruptive passengers to be quiet, and to sit down. When we do this exercise with individuals, and with groups, it's the same thing. Turn around and argue with the passengers just like a real bus driver. So, feel free to really get involved in the argument if you can. Some people find it difficult to argue with the passengers. Whatever you experience, try to be aware of it.

Make sure you address all of the passengers you chose for the avoidance exercise.

When you have finished this exercise, once again think about what it was like. Was it easy to argue with the passengers? Did you enjoy it? How did you feel arguing with them? Once again, write down your answers to these questions.

Some people enjoy arguing with the passengers. It can make them feel strong, or in control. Other people hate it. It brings up very strong emotions; they can feel on the spot, threatened, and not in control at all. There is no right or wrong response, or better or worse way to react. Different monsters/passengers do different things to different people; that is all. Some of the aims of the exercises that make up Monsters on the Bus is to become aware of the monsters, how we react to them, and what our most familiar or habitual patterns of responding to them tend to be.

The most crucial part of engaging in arguing with the passengers is noticing where your attention was when you were disputing with them. Were you facing towards your values (the way you should have been facing)? Were you aware of them? Were you aware of what was in the room in the direction of your values? Or, was your attention directed towards the passengers rather than the road you are on?

Exercise Three – Acknowledge/Accept

We will try a different tack for this exercise.

Just as in the previous two exercises, sit or stand facing the direction that represents moving towards your values. Call the unruly disruptive passengers to mind one at a time. Say their negative comments. Remember to try to become aware of the feelings they generate. Your task for this exercise is simply to hear what each passenger is saying. Feel the effect it has on you without resistance. Fully allow those feelings. This means that you do not avoid or fight against them. This also means no smiling, grimacing, or making faces. Fully accepting what has been said does not make it true, or real. It does allow you to listen, though, and to fully feel the effect of these thoughts or beliefs.

When you have fully attended to what a passenger has said, acknowledge that you have heard it. When we do this exercise with people in a workshop, the 'monster' is played by another person, and the acknowledgment takes the form of lightly laying your hand on their shoulder to show you have heard what was said. It is important not to rush the acknowledgment. Many people want to sweep the passenger aside, and almost push it away. When doing this exercise on your own, you can reach up and lay your hand on your own shoulder, on the top or front of the shoulder (not the side) to show your acknowledgement. Repeat this for all the passengers you chose for the first exercise.

This is a difficult exercise.

Willingly allowing negative comments about ourselves, and the very real emotions that go with them, is not easy. People are often quiet and thoughtful after doing this exercise. Although the emotions felt during the exercise have gone, there seem to be reverberations in the stillness afterwards. Use this time to review the exercise.

When you did this exercise, how did you feel? Was it easy to allow the feelings? What were those feelings? Where were they in the body? Be specific by going into the detail we asked you to be aware of in earlier chapters, when recording your reactions.

How did this feel compared to the other ways of dealing with the passengers we talked about – avoiding, arguing? Was it easy or hard? Which of the three ways felt most familiar to you? Which way were you facing when you were acknowledging this monster? What were you aware of? Were you more aware of your valued activities, or of the passenger?

Exercise Four – Action

This time, we would like you to stand facing your valued direction. Briefly bring to mind what the life you are heading for is like. Once again, bring the passengers to mind. Imagine them standing right behind you, with all of them talking at the same time. They are all shouting at you, putting you down, wanting you to avoid things, saying your dreams are foolish and unrealistic; you haven't got time to do the things you want, you're not good enough, there is no point.

For a few moments, give the passengers free rein. Let that negativity flow. If you can, say some of their comments out loud, or record them on your phone and play them back while you stand there. Try to fully allow the feelings these comments bring up and, while doing that, see if you can take a step forward in the direction of the life you value.

When doing this, try not to 'push through' or rush the exercise by temporarily shutting the passengers down and just taking a step. Like the previous exercise, see if you can actively attend to your passengers without avoiding, arguing, or agreeing with them. Then, see if you can take one conscious step in the direction of your valued life. If you can take one step, can you take two? You don't have to take a step forward, but we suggest you try – just to see what it is like and what you can do.

Take a few minutes to review this exercise. Could you take a step? Write a few words describing your experience. Then answer these questions. How did this exercise compare to the others, Avoid, Argue, and Accept? Was it more difficult, or easier? Of the four exercises you have just done, which felt the most familiar? Is this your habitual way of dealing with your passengers? Which exercise was most difficult? Which of the four ways of dealing with your passengers will help take you towards living the life you want?

Some thoughts on Monsters on the Bus

The Monsters on the Bus exercises embody all the components of ACT. Doing the exercises requires you to be aware of your values; that is the starting point. Framing negative thoughts and beliefs as Passengers or Monsters (i.e., separate from yourself) is a form of defusion from your thoughts. Allowing these negative thoughts, and being aware of the emotions that go with them, is certainly acceptance and being in contact with the present moment; that is, with your current experience.

The whole experience – seeing a valued life, moving towards it, imagining yourself as the driver of a bus with various passengers – allows you to see yourself in context, as part of a process, rather than as a single fixed idea. The simple act of engaging in the exercise is committed action; action that moves you towards the type of life you want. Monsters on the Bus is a microcosm of ACT in that doing it – rather than simply thinking about it – means that you are Open, Aware, and Engaged.

Remembering these exercises, and being aware of how it felt engaging with your passengers in different ways, can help you to notice these habits of reacting in everyday situations. We have also practised skills relevant to all the ACT processes. So, now you know from experience that you can accept unwanted feelings and thoughts. You can feel them, they don't kill you, and they fade and change. They even go away. You know you can move towards what you want, even though it is difficult. You have done it in the past.

Unfortunately, just as in any sport, one good training session does not make you a master. Committed action means committing (doing something) again, and again, and again. We will be referring back to the Monsters on the Bus and your particular passengers as we look at ways of dealing with specific problems such as performance anxiety, motivation, and perfectionism.

Before we look at how to deal with particular issues, we will introduce you to another exercise that will help you become more open, aware, and engaged in the midst of daily activity. It develops awareness, acceptance, defusion, and (of course) involves committed action. This is an important exercise. It builds on the mindfulness exercises we have already done, and serves as a foundation from which we will develop further exercises for dealing with specific problems. It has the very exciting title of Diary of Reactive Habits.

Diary of Reactive Habits

The Diary of Reactive Habits, as we use it in this book, is based on the work of Dr. Bruno Cayoun.

This exercise was developed as part of Dr. Cayoun's Mindfulness Integrated Cognitive Behavioural Therapy (MiCBT). We will use the Diary of Reactive Habits as a way to help you:

1. Notice where you are directing your attention
2. Increase your awareness of bodily sensations
3. Defuse, and become less entangled with your thoughts
4. Increase awareness of avoidance
5. Increase awareness of physical reality; your five senses

If you look at the figure on the next page, you will see it contains a record form. This is similar to the forms you have filled out earlier when recording your experiences. It has five boxes. The aim is to record your reactions in different situations. These can be instances when you have a big reaction (like getting very angry, or really nervous) or small everyday annoyances that you quickly forget (like spilling something at the table when eating, or dropping a fork on the floor). We will explain more about why to do this, but first we will go through what should be recorded in each box.

1. **Situation (Internal or External)**
   This is the situation you are in, or a triggering event. Internal refers to something inside, like a memory, a thought, or a physical feeling. A physical feeling might be something like a pain in your leg during a race, or noticing that your heart is beating really fast before an event.

2. **Sensory Perception**
   This is anything that comes from outside the body. Anything you see, hear, taste, feel through touch, or smell. In other words, physical reality; what is around you at the time of the event.

3. **Evaluation (Thoughts, Judgements, Images).**
   This is what goes through your head. What we might call 'mental stuff'. These are the thoughts that flow on from the situation,

or a triggering event. These include your evaluations about the situation, or bodily sensations, predictions about the future, memories, plans, and images.

4. Bodily Sensations

This is simply sensations in the body. These are sensory sensations, but come from the body rather than being driven from outside. If I touch the table, I feel something. For our purposes, that is 'sensory perception'. If I have a tightness in my chest, or a blocked nose, that is a bodily sensation. It is primarily internal.

5. Reaction/Response

This is what you do. It is your reaction to the situation. This includes anything you do physically. Anything that a video might pick up, or that someone watching would be able to see. It can also include plans, memories, or stories you tell yourself beyond the more immediate thoughts associated with the event.

We will run through a couple of examples to give you an idea of how this works in practice, and how to fill out the record sheets. In these examples, we will use fictional people, but they are based on real situations we have encountered. The examples are based on an amalgamation of the experiences of several individuals, including ourselves.

Example One

In example one, we will look at the experience of Dave, a golfer. Dave's problem was that when he played on his own, he performed well, with low scores. But in club competition, he was much worse. Every time he competed, his score would be 15 to 20 strokes worse. He said he got nervous when playing with others, but only in competition. This didn't happen when he played practice rounds with one or two good friends. You could say that, in this instance, Dave's Nervous Passenger was getting in the way of his playing. Dave was asked to think about the last time he played in the club competition and produced a bad shot. He closed his eyes and imagined himself back in the situation and recalled what happened. You can see his reactions in the figure.

If you look at the situation Dave recorded, he was teeing off at the start of a hole. What he mainly noticed was his thoughts and evaluations. He has quite a few things written down under Evaluation. It normally takes a bit of prompting to get people to remember as much as possible, but if you mentally walk yourself through the situation you are recalling, more things come up. He also had a good recall of what he did. If you look at the other two boxes, Bodily Sensations and Sensory Perceptions, there is hardly anything. He recorded one item under Bodily Sensations, and nothing at all under Sensory Perception.

Diary of Reactive Habits

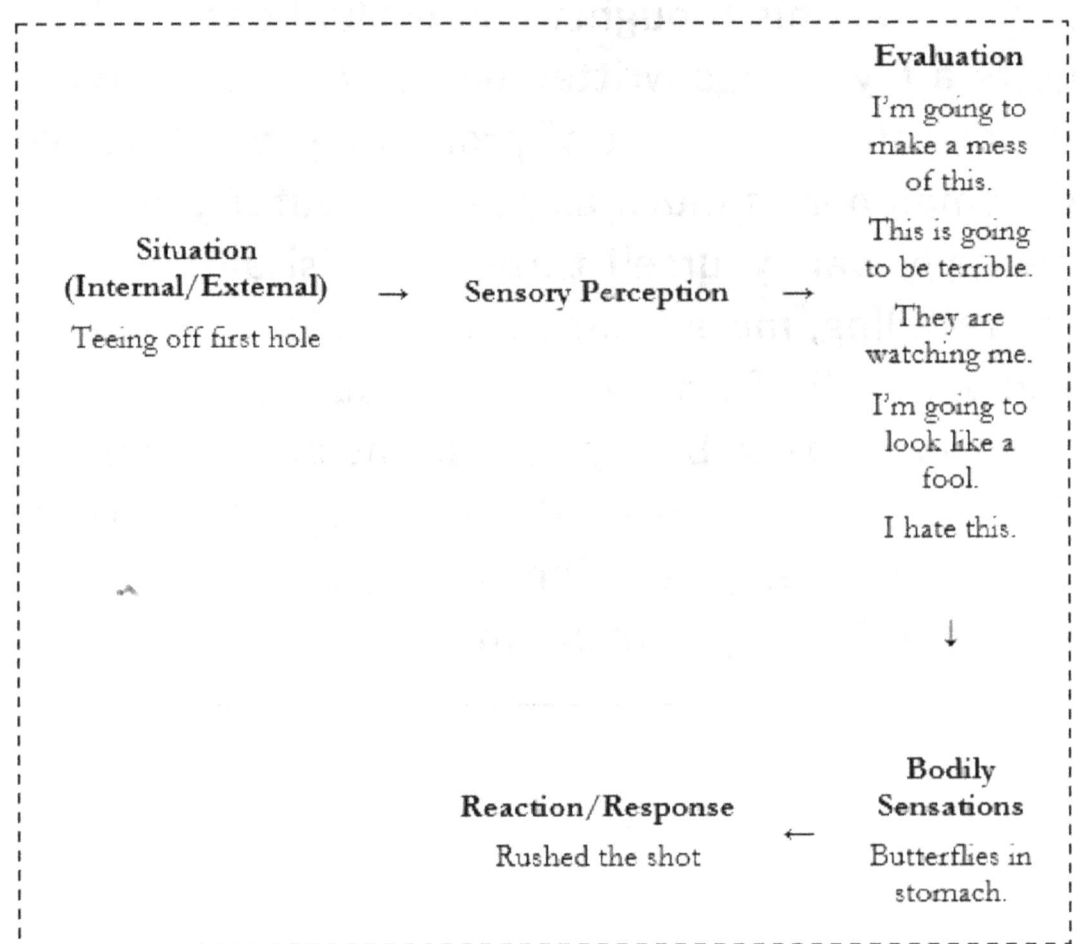

Sensory perceptions refer to what you noticed at the time. If pressed, Dave would say things like 'I must have seen the ball', 'the grass must have been green', 'I would have seen my club', but that is not what he was aware of at the time. At the time, his attention was on his evaluations, judgements, and thoughts, and on his responses to them; not on most of physical reality. That is, he was not focusing on what was around him, and what was going on in his body. He was aware of some things in his body, but only the most extreme physical sensations. He then interpreted them as 'I'm nervous', 'This is going to be terrible' and so on. Which only made him more nervous and fuelled more thoughts about his situation.

Dave's responses are pretty typical. Most people are aware of the type of things that go through their heads in a stressful situation, and of what they do. They are normally much less aware of what is going on in their body, and on what is around them. People literally aren't aware of what is in front of them 'in the moment' when their attention is narrowed and focused inward on their thinking.

One of the aims of this exercise is to develop the ability to pay more attention to your own bodily sensations and sensory perceptions, what is actually going on, and less attention to thoughts, evaluations, and planning your responses to things. In general, people's responses take care of themselves. They tend to be pretty automatic and vary with the circumstances. In turning down the volume of the internal monologue and of our evaluations, and turning up the volume of the awareness of physical reality, our negative passengers have less impact on our behaviour. It is our behaviour that determines our performance.

Example Two

Mary has had a long layoff from running and is getting back into training. A major hurdle for her is that she doesn't like people seeing her run. She feels slow and is embarrassed she is so slow. She has also put on weight and is embarrassed at how she looks when running. Mary recounted one instance when she was running up a hill and saw her shadow. She said, 'I couldn't believe I was that old fat person barely moving up the hill.' Mary doesn't want people to see her running, but it has been an important part of her life. As a result, Mary only runs at certain times, and in certain places. This severely limits her training as she does not simply leave the house for a run, and doesn't feel comfortable running to and from work. Mary filled out the diary in relation to one time she did go for a run from home. You can see her responses in the following figure.

Diary of Reactive Habits

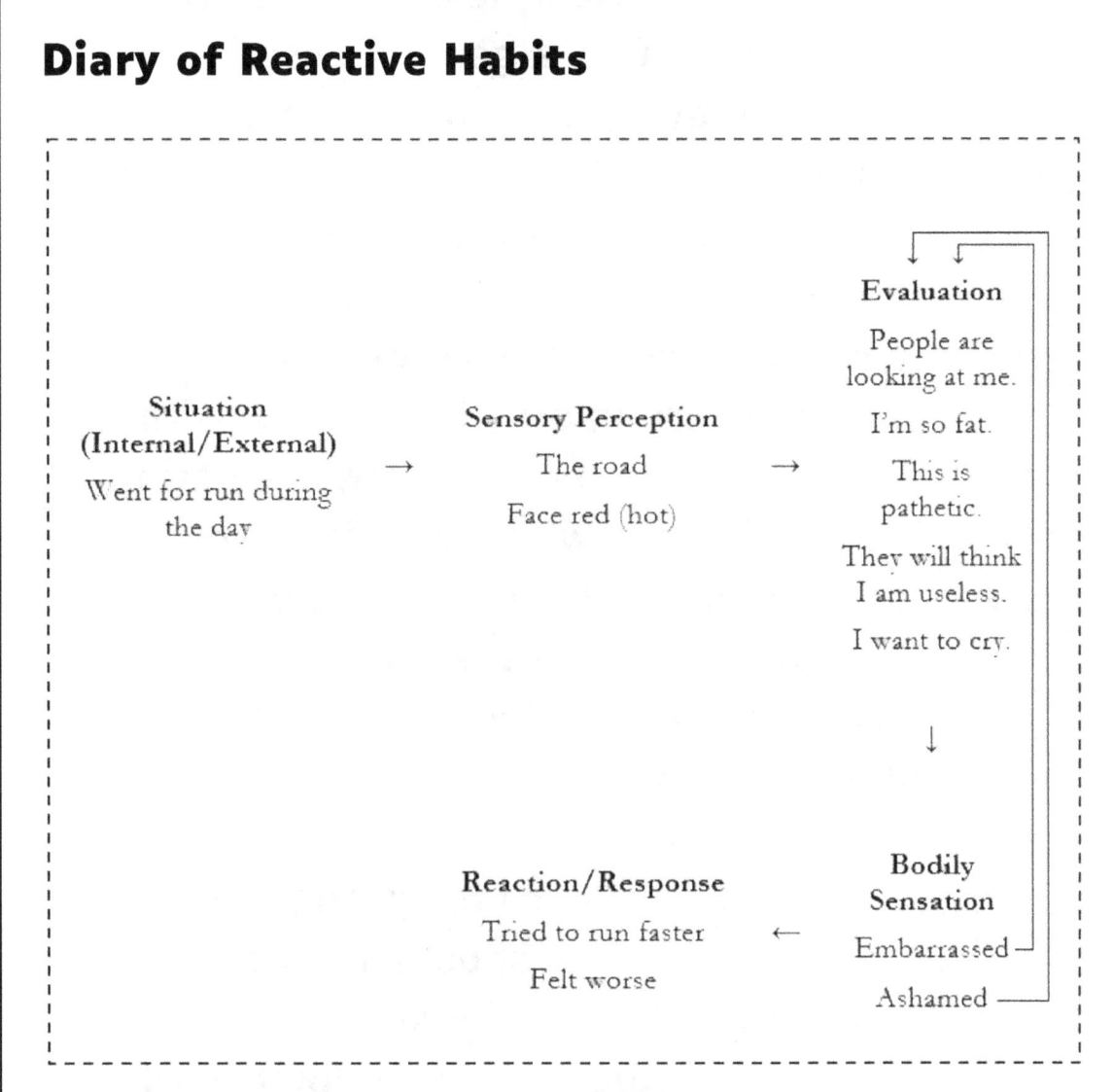

Like Dave, Mary has a lot under evaluations/judgements, and not a lot in the Bodily Sensation category. If you look at the figure, you will see that we have drawn arrows from 'embarrassed' and 'ashamed' in the Sensation section to the box for Evaluations. Mary said she felt ashamed; however, this is not a clear description of what she felt in her body. It is a general description of an emotion. In everyday conversation, saying you are embarrassed or ashamed are very good descriptions – people know what you mean – but we need to be more specific here. These general terms are really describing a series of sensations we experience in certain situations along with certain thoughts. They are, in effect, evaluations or judgements about how we feel. We want to explore, or turn up the volume on the physical sensations that relate to these broad emotions, and pay less attention to the verbal evaluations of these bodily sensations.

In Mary's case, she felt her face getting hot, cringing a bit, drawing her shoulders in or forward, and feeling sick in the stomach. When you are using the record form, you don't need to relate specific sensations to certain thoughts or emotions in the diary. It is useful though to notice when you experience an emotion like embarrassment or anger and to attend to the body and notice what you feel. What are the physical sensations? In Mary's case, regarding feeling 'sick in the stomach', we would ask her:

'Where do you feel sick in the stomach?'

'How big an area does it cover? . . . Show me.'

'Does it feel sharp or dull?'

'Is it hot or cold?'

'Heavy or light?'

'Does it move?'

'Is it different in the centre compared to the edges?'

'Is it near the skin or deeper in?'

It is helpful to look at sensations like hot or cold, sharp or dull, as on a continuum. Not as all or nothing. If it helps, you can draw a line on the back of the form with one end representing hot, and the other cold, and mark roughly where your experience sits along this line. You could also hold both hands up in front of you (about a shoulder's width apart) and make a judgement like that. The aim is to increase your awareness of the sensation, and its intensity. Descriptors like 'It was terrible' or 'I hated it' don't describe the sensation itself. They are thoughts, or judgements. You can probably see that such descriptions only serve to increase the idea of how bad it was, and the desire to avoid it in the future.

What we are doing by this process is investigating our automatic reactions; this includes our emotions, and the words or ideas we use to describe how we feel. Increasing our awareness of how we actually feel – awareness of the physical sensations we experience – helps us defuse from our thoughts about these feelings. As a result, we become less driven by internal events (thoughts and emotions) and more able to respond flexibly to the situation in front of us. We see the thoughts that arise not as 'me', or even accurate descriptions of 'me', but as separate aspects of an experience. This makes us more Open and Aware regarding these experiences, and allows us to avoid unhelpful automatic or reactive responding, as we move towards our valued behaviour.

On Mary's form, you might notice that she described her face as red, and I have added in brackets 'hot'. This is an example of how some descriptors are evaluations or judgements, and not sensations. When Mary was running, she didn't have a mirror to look at her face to see that it was red. Even if she did, 'red' is a description, not a sensation. When using this record sheet, review what you are writing and try to be as clear as possible in describing what you feel in the body, and what is a judgement regarding that feeling.

Sensory Perception

Recording sensory perceptions – what comes to our five senses from outside the body – is something people typically struggle with at first. Most people have five senses, so it is not a lack of sensory ability. It is a lack of having developed the ability to attend.

Not attending is normal. We don't attend a lot of the time. It is not uncommon to be reading something and drift off into thinking about something else. When that happens, we can be unaware of the page in front of us; even though our eyes are open. We can blank out when someone is talking to us, and we can operate on automatic pilot when driving, not being aware of a lot around us. It is quite an amazing ability to be conscious, with all our senses working, and not be aware of what is going on! It doesn't seem to be a useful ability in terms of dealing with current circumstances, but is amazing nonetheless. In a sporting context, zoning out can not only be unproductive in terms of performance, but in some circumstances can be dangerous.

As we have said previously, by using this record sheet (the Diary of Reactive Habits), we hope to turn up the awareness of the five senses, and of what is happening in the physical world, as opposed to having your primary focus being on your imagination or evaluations. By recording several instances a day, you will be forced to consider what is around you, and to take note of it. This is a simple adjunct to your mindfulness practice. It takes mindfulness into your activities. The awareness of 'what is', without adding anything extra. Some examples of sensory perceptions as I write this are:

- Light coming in, on my left side, glaring into my left eye
- Heat and tingling on my left forearm from the sun
- The hum of the computer
- Fingers on the keyboard
- Small black speakers on either side of my computer screen. Smooth on top, a mesh pattern on the front
- A computer screen with coloured shapes along the bottom: red, yellow, blue, orange, red and white box shapes
- The sound of wind against the house and something rattling
- A white phone charger on top of a black notebook
- The weight of my legs on my chair, and my feet on the floor

Things to practise

We suggest you fill out a Diary of Reactive Habits sheet, three times a day, for five days. Fill out at least one every day of the week if you can.

When recording your reactions, it is good to use instances of when your monsters/passengers show up and get in the way. It is also very useful to practise using ordinary experiences. Simple things that don't seem to be a major issue. You make a cup of coffee, and it gets cold before you get around to drinking it; you get held up in traffic and get annoyed; or your partner or a friend says something you don't like. You can also use more positive experiences. If you come home and your dog is happy to see you, how does it feel? What do you notice? What goes through your head? It is important to record these everyday occurrences. Breaking down your experiences for both small and large events will develop greater awareness, and openness to experience, and foster defusion from unwanted or controlling thoughts. However, this is also a stepping stone, a building of skills towards extending this and other exercises that will help you deal with your own unruly passengers.

Summary

- This chapter introduced the idea of Monsters/Passengers on the Bus. This is a way of seeing our negative habits of thinking, and reacting to situations as passengers (or monsters) that travel with us, as we move towards the type of life we want.

- If we try to avoid these passengers, and their unruly behaviour, or focus on them as something to get rid of, we are diverted from fully engaging in those things that are important to us.

- Developing an awareness of our own individual passengers, and the effect they can have on us, allows us to develop effective methods of dealing with them.

- Using the Diary of Reactive Habits record sheet is an extension of mindfulness practice and builds towards dealing with these unwanted experiences in the midst of activity.

- Using a Diary of Reactive Habits record sheet, we practised increasing our awareness of the physical sensations we experience in the presence of our unwanted passengers, plus awareness of the objective reality of our five senses; what is happening to and around us.

- By paying more attention to our physical sensations, we effectively turn down the volume of our internal thoughts. That is, our habitual evaluations, and imaginings, along with paying less attention to planning our responses to situations. We are, in effect, defusing or loosening the grip of very powerful negative patterns of thinking, while becoming more open, aware, and engaged in our activities.

We will continue to refer to the Monsters on the Bus as we look at ways of dealing with specific problems; for example, performance anxiety, lack of motivation, and loss of focus. We will also use the skills developed by practising mindful awareness, and filling in the Diary of Reactive Habits as we introduce other exercises to deal with these problems. In the next chapter, we will look specifically at anxiety, how it impacts on performance, and ways we can deal with the most common barrier to performance.

Chapter 5

THE ANXIOUS PASSENGER

Anxious passengers can range from low-key guests that make you feel slightly nervous, to scary-looking monsters that make your stomach turn and give you sleepless nights. For many athletes, these are the most difficult passengers to deal with. In some situations, the most troubling monsters can threaten the very essence of who you think you are. They seem to target us where we are most vulnerable, threatening to expose what we see as our weaknesses. So, let's go and check them out more closely.

Often, athletes and coaches believe that if fear and angst could just be switched off, then performance would be smooth and improve, in a sort of unhindered way.

Wayne is a bit like that. He'll have some doubt about his performance tomorrow, and he'll try hard to put it out of his mind. The night before a match, he'll be tempted to maybe have a beer to dampen the nagging thoughts and feel a bit better; but his coach has said not to, so he will try to watch a movie and tune out.

These distraction techniques help for a little while, then the doom and gloom monsters catch him out again when he is in bed. He can't have sex tonight because his coach said that is not a good idea either, which leaves him with the same problem; it is like trying to ban the elephant from your mind in the small exercise we did in the Introduction chapter.

The result is a lot of tossing and turning and little sleep.

The next day he feels a bit irritable but he tells himself to 'stay positive' and that things will work out alright. This all seems a bit laboured, even to Wayne, but he believes that this is probably because he hasn't practised staying calm and positive enough yet.

Trying not to think negative thoughts

When – during the match the next day – a player from another team tackles Wayne a bit hard, he has had enough. His ability to contain his inner turmoil has reached its limit; he reacts, and gets a red card.

We all know people who try to deal with unwelcome inner experiences in a similar way. We only have to look in the mirror in most cases. Avoiding and trying to control unwelcome inner experiences is still the most common way we react to them.

Anxiety and the humanmind

Let's look at what is happening here more closely. Experiencing 'anxiety' is the result of your interpretation of a situation. If that signals danger to you, it usually goes hand-in-hand with increased levels of physiological arousal. This means you will experience high levels of physical activation such as your heart rate increasing, muscles tensing, and (at times) even shivering. This combination of your interpretation of what might be happening, or could happen, and the increased activity in your body, will lead to you to experience feelings, such as 'anxiety', 'panic', or 'fear'.

Often, this cluster of things happening will amplify each other: they include the actual events, your interpretations or thoughts about these events, your feelings, your thoughts about your feelings, the sensations in your body, and again your interpretation of them.

For example, one thought that starts things off for Wayne might be, 'If I don't perform well in this match I might be out of the team'. Then, of course, he is aware of this thought, and the body reactions that go with it and other thoughts follow: 'Oh damn, now I am feeling anxious. Shit, this will make it really hard, I should be relaxed and confident'. This again leads to more emotional and physical reactions in his body that he doesn't like. And, with Wayne being Wayne, he would like to get rid of these as quickly as possible.

Don't we all? For most of us, this is a normal way of reacting. These feelings and thoughts are something we don't like, and we almost intuitively respond to them in the same way we do with things we don't like in the outer world. It's as if there is a sudden strange smell in your kitchen; it's unpleasant and you try to figure out where it's coming from, and then how to get rid of it. For this purpose, your mind serves you well. Usually, you succeed. Unfortunately, we have to tell you that you can't get rid of these inner experiences in the same way you can get rid of dog poo. If you read the first chapter, you might already understand why. If you skipped it, here is a summary.

Due to our ability to have language-based thinking, we try to think our way out of things. This is a good thing if there is a problem in the world outside our skin. The other team plays the game in a certain way and we have to find a new way to respond to this, tactically. We apply analysis and logic, and our ability to think is a great asset.

Applying the same logic to our inner world doesn't always work, though. We can't think our way out of having thoughts we don't like (e.g., thoughts of doubt or worries about failing). There are several reasons for this. One is that any thought of 'not having x', with 'x' being the 'pink elephant' or 'thought of failing in competition' etc., already contains the x you don't want. You might try the following experiment with the elephant image again, to get an understanding of why a control strategy like stopping your thoughts, or 'getting rid of' anxiety, might not work. Get a stopwatch out and try hard for 20 seconds NOT to think of a pink elephant. Imagine that your life hinges on you NOT thinking of one. Now...

What happened? Usually the following happens... in our experience, 80 % of people cannot avoid thinking of the pink elephant for 20 seconds, while 20 % avoid the thought of a pink elephant by thinking very hard about a green elephant or something similar. Were you successful in avoiding thoughts of the pink elephant like the 20 %? Well, don't get excited yet! First of all, this was a 20-second exercise and, like so many strategies, it can work in the short run.

Would it have worked for 20 minutes? Probably not. Let's assume someone could muster enough effort and concentration to keep a pink elephant out of their mind for a long time. Would this serve them well in a sporting situation (or any situation in life)? Let's assume they would be even more skilled, and push that negative thought away with 'positive thinking'.

How would this affect their game? What you would be doing is spending all of your capacity for attention and thinking trying not to think of something 'negative'. You are mentally holding shut the door on that 'pink elephant thought' using a 'green elephant'. That's very clever. Almost as clever as shutting out negative thoughts with positive thoughts. However, all you are doing is narrowing your attention to your own little battle in your own head. And you do this while the rest of your team tries hard to play a game. The game you should be spending attention on, right now. While you narrow your attention in this way, what is actually called for is a broad, open, engaged attention to the game you are playing.

And for the same reason, it doesn't work if you try to 'not want', or 'fight', unwanted feelings or bodily sensations like butterflies in your tummy. This is easier to understand with the following metaphor.

Imagine that you are sitting on a flipping chair that is placed on top of a shark tank. You are wired up to all sorts of monitors that record your heart rate, galvanic skin response, and other indicators of physical activation, or anxiety. Someone tells you that the moment you get anxious, this will show up on the monitors, and as soon as your anxiety reaches a certain level, the chair will flip and you will end up in the shark tank.

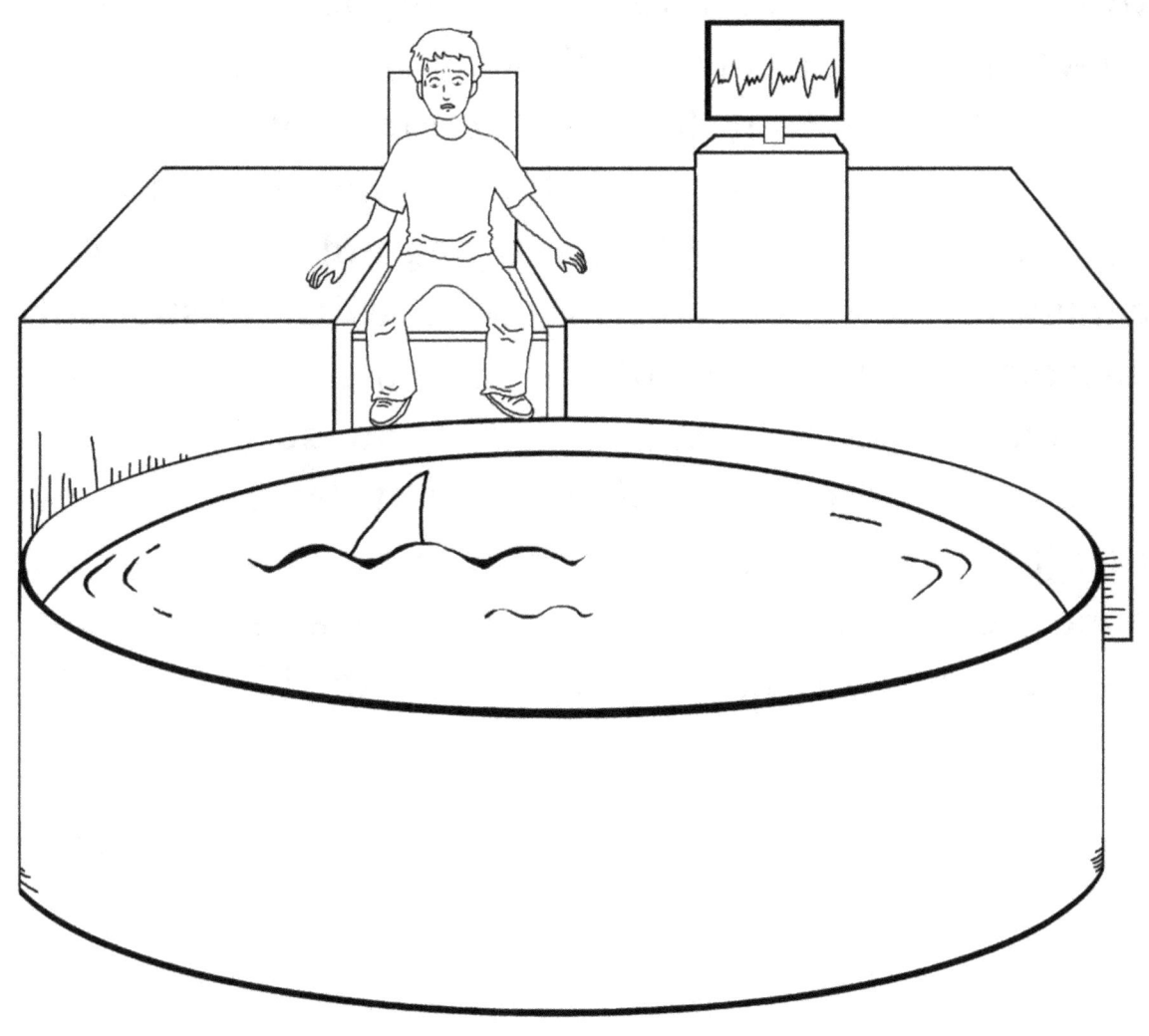

What do you think will happen?

Yeah, we think that too. Because, most likely, what you will try to do is what most people have traditionally been told to do: try to get rid of any anxiety or nervousness; better still, try not to have it in the first place.

In this example, what you are trying not to have is a feeling, and the physiological sensations that go hand in hand with it. So, what you most likely do is carefully monitor your body for any vague possible sign of the sensation you are trying not to have! A benign niggle somewhere in your body could suddenly become the messenger of the early signs of anxiety. You know what anxiety means for you, so you try not to pay attention to it and suppress it; by trying to do this (in a roundabout way), you are actually doing the opposite... you are paying much more attention to it, and suddenly you are face-to-face with this:

The process of paying attention to physical sensations, paired with specific interpretations of them, amplifies these sensations. Even imagining a physiological sensation can bring it about and make it bigger. This is a process that hypnosis makes use of, and that has often been shown in placebo effects in medicine. Certain outcomes are suggested, you start to expect them, you monitor your body for subtle signs of them, and by paying attention (in a certain, expectant way), you bring these experiences about and enlarge them.

A Study on the effects of Acceptance and Control

In 2003, Eifert and Heffner conducted an experiment to compare the effects of an 'acceptance versus control stance to uncomfortable physical experiences'. A group of women who scored high on sensitivity to anxiety was asked to breathe carbon dioxide-enriched air, which usually produces sensations similar to those experienced in a panic attack.

One group of women was taught to accept and not to fight their 'symptoms'.

> Women in the second group were taught a breathing skill and asked to try to use the breathing skill in order to control their symptoms – an 'intervention' somewhat akin to some traditional 'mental skills' taught since the 1980s. Nearly half of the women in the latter group were worried about losing control, and almost 20 % did.
>
> The women in the 'acceptance group' reported less intense fear, and fewer catastrophic thoughts (i.e., they did not worry about losing control). By giving up efforts to control their discomfort they – paradoxically – were less affected by it.

In ACT, there is a term for what most of us are trying to do with unpleasant inner happenings: Experiential Avoidance.

Classic examples of this might relate to the 'fear of spiders', and the fear of speaking in front of large groups of people. What do most people feel an urge to do in these situations, especially if it is a strong fear for them? They want to get rid of the feeling! And if they fail in their attempts to switch off their discomfort, they make some excuse, and don't face the situation they are afraid of: they avoid.

The term 'experiential avoidance', however, points to what is at the core of our dislike and discomfort: our inner **experience** that is triggered by the outer challenge. It is not the 'spider', per se, that we don't want and avoid, nor the large group of people we are meant to speak to – what we are really avoiding is our own inner discomfort in this feared situation. This distinction is important, because it means that as you become better at tolerating or accepting inner discomfort, your need to avoid outer situations diminishes. Or, in short, avoidance limits our range of behaviours, and acceptances broadens it.

Of course, we can avoid the spider, or the group of people. Our brain is good at coming up with excuses and ways not to meet these challenges. And the more it does this 'successfully', the better it gets at the skill of avoidance. However, in doing this, your passengers or fears remain, they are there to haunt you again next time. Your habitual avoidance is likely to make them even stronger.

The metaphor of a hungry tiger (Hayes, 2005) illustrates the dangers of continued avoidance. Imagine that, one day, you find a hungry baby tiger on your doorstep. You take it in, it demands some food, and you go to the fridge, find something and feed it. The tiger cub calms down; all is good. Until it wakes up again, slightly stronger and bigger, and demands more food. You want to keep it quiet, so you get some more food from the supermarket; baby tiger is happy, and you are happy... and so on and so on.

Weeks go by, and the same cycle keeps repeating, just that the tiger is not a baby anymore, it has become stronger and more assertive, and if it asks for more food now, you do not really have much choice in the matter. You'd better go and get some quickly.

The more you keep your inner tiger happy, the bigger it will get. Your life becomes much narrower in many ways and ruled by your increasing efforts to contain the tiger. Effort also means time and attention, and by now we should know that when you play any sport, your attention should not be given to anything but what you are supposed to focus on in the moment of competition!

There are numerous examples of how this avoidance behaviour plays out, in more or less subtle ways, when athletes come for psychological consultation. The golfer who rushes his next shot in order to avoid the discomfort caused by a recent mistake and the anxiety not to make another one. The rugby player who does not put himself out for a pass with the same determination he would usually have, for fear of fumbling the ball once again. The long-distance runner who seeks excuses for not doing so well in the middle of the race, or the swimmer who puts in only 80 % – knowing that this will help him rationalise why he did not win the race.

These more or less subtle ways of avoiding the discomfort one faces, or might have to face in the future, happen all the time. To gain back some ground from avoidance, first you need to be aware of these old tricks your passengers play on you. And, next, you need to have clarity of values and direction, and courage to take the wheel back into your own hands.

"I did not take this penalty because I did not feel confident enough today."

"I did not train well, today. I felt a bit lazy and unmotivated."

"I gave it only 70% today. I could win if I tried."

"If I fake an injury, people might not be so critical of me."

Wayne being busy trying to preserve his equilibrium

In short, a sportsman like Wayne would be busy thinking up excuses for avoiding inner discomfort (e.g., anxiety, shame, frustration, guilt and whatever else might show up to him during a difficult match).

Some, like Conrad, would instead turn to focus on the kind of person he wants to be, (i.e., what the situation calls for, in line with his values). He might focus on showing courage to his opponent, even in the face of his inner passengers, and play the best tennis match he can. His attention will be on the things that matter in relation to the match he is in right now, and not at all on what he could come up with later, after he lost (e.g., to preserve his self-esteem and not make himself feel quite so bad). If you read this book in sequence and did the exercises in our chapter on Values, you know what you will need to focus on when your passengers are eagerly trying to get you off track.

Too busy with the situation to wonder about the excuses he might have later.

What could someone like Wayne do to become a bit more like Conrad?

To understand this better, try to think about what someone has to do when caught in Chinese handcuffs (also known as the Chinese finger trap).

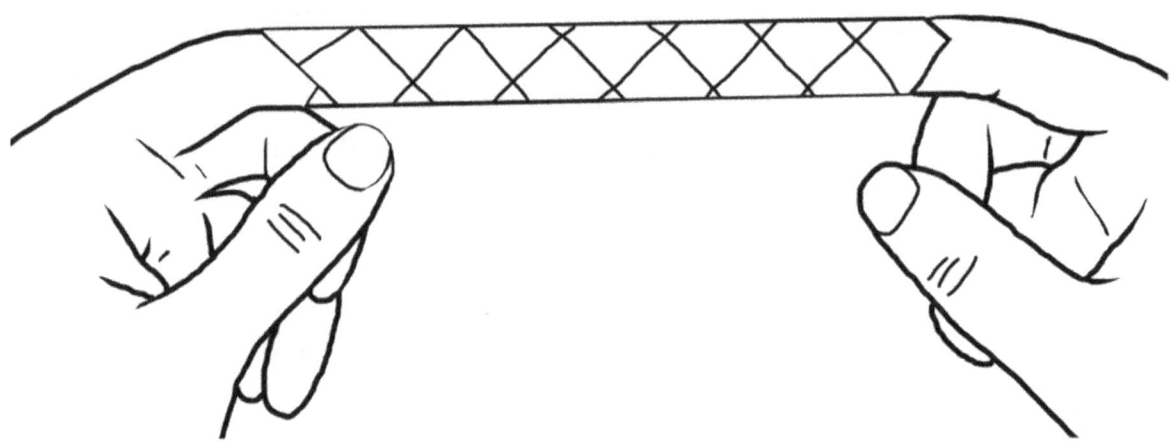

The more you try to pull out of Chinese handcuffs, the tighter they get, and the more you feel trapped. In that sense, it is similar to the feeding of the baby tiger mentioned earlier. It makes the situation worse.

The solution is to 'Go in!' Doing the opposite of what is usually the automatic response and pulling away. With the Chinese finger trap, by pushing in, you loosen the weave in the trap and you can escape. In a similar way, you can lean into your experiences and face them. By doing this, you would get some wiggle room; you are not constrained by your fears or habits and get some room to move. (Chinese Handcuffs metaphor, Hayes & Smith, 2005).

In a nutshell. Trying to control unpleasant inner experiences not only doesn't work, but it also becomes the problem. **Avoidance** behaviour is one form of attempting to gain control. Avoidance does not work because it amplifies the original issue by giving it too much headspace, quite literally. In any sporting situation, athletes who have little tolerance, or **acceptance of** inner discomfort are often tempted to pay more attention to trying to 'not feel bad' than to the relevant sporting stimuli. And thus, due to our limited attentional capacities, especially in a high-performance situation, they are likely to pay too little attention to relevant stimuli in their environment.

A study on 'Catastrophic Performance Decline'

Edwards, Kingston, Hardy, and Gould (2002) studied the sudden declines in the performances of a number of athletes.

> Results suggested that when athletes shifted their attention from game-related information to their internal stimuli, e.g., their own self-evaluation of their performances, then this often became one factor that led to what they termed 'catastrophic performance decline'.

It's important to note that we are not advocating a complete absence of attention to inner processes. But, when athletes perform at their best, there are often automatic and subtle changes in the processes of awareness, similar to those occurring when a state of 'Flow' is achieved.

In Flow, there is an adaptive attention to internal and external processes that are important for the task at hand, rather than an excessive self-focus and (importantly) self-talk that occurs in the anxious athlete who is constantly evaluating how things are going. The Diary of Reactive Habits in Chapter 4 is one way you can begin to learn to become aware of your own self-talk, and to defuse from it.

What does all this mean? We all have what we have called 'monsters': negative thoughts, fears, and unwanted emotions that get in the way of our performance. The best way to deal with them is to face them. Like a master Samurai, perhaps, who is not so much fearless as totally engaged in the task at hand. That can be playing with a puppy, or standing with sword raised prepared to fight. And what we want to encourage you to do is to pay attention, and to take **engaged action**.

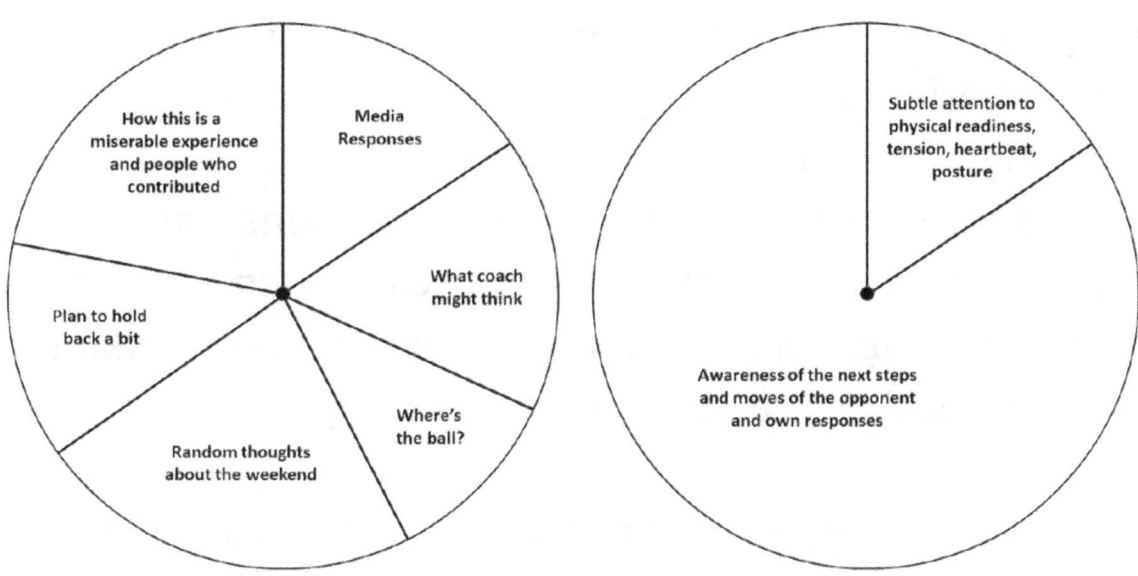

Wayne's mind content before a penalty, and Conrad's mind content before a tennis match

It is similar to the process we described with the baby tiger, but in a more positive direction. The more you feed that ability to engage, the willingness to accept, and to face your most difficult passengers, the stronger you become. Other situations that life throws up become like a training ground for your sport, when you practise building attention, willingness, acceptance, and the ability to be fully engaged in your activities.

We are facing two interacting struggles at the same time, an inner and an outer one. Facing a dreaded situation in your sport, (e.g., your last attempt at a high jump in a competition), will bring up the very experiences you might be tempted to avoid. Challenging situations are mostly difficult because of what we experience inside, our emotions and the thoughts and stories that go with them. To the outer challenge, we can bring our usual mental skills: tactical decisions, a game plan, strategy.

But we also have to respond to the inner struggle. We must decide if we are going to face a situation and do what we need to do, or if we avoid our discomfort and choose what appears to be a comfortable path.

While we say you must choose, we assume that – on the big picture level – you have already made a choice with regards to the role of your sport in your life. And, if you think about it, it should be clear what choice you need to make in this very moment. One day, when you look back on your sporting life, you won't be proud about feeling comfortable and never having challenged yourself. People usually remember the tough games, the hard races, and the trickiest challenges they stood up to. And it's not only about what will have mattered to you when looking back! These most difficult situations are essential for making you the athlete you want to be. They are not only challenges you need to learn to cope with; they are struggles you need to have in order to discover the limits of your potential and your optimal performances.

If you don't really believe that being challenged and being willing to fail again and again is necessary to improve, then take a minute and try to think of any great athlete who became what he or she is without doing so?

To become an outstanding athlete, you will have to accept that challenges and failures are part and parcel of your journey. They are sitting right there, on your path. You will meet them like the driver of the bus you met in the previous chapter, who is driving along on his chosen path in spite of all his nasty passengers trying to get him off track. Michael Jordan has famously summarised this fact for himself:

'I've missed more than 9,000 shots in my career. I've lost almost 300 games. 26 times, I've been trusted to take the game winning shot and missed. I've failed over and over and over again in my life. And that is why I succeed.'

Developing Acceptance and Courage

There are a number of training exercises you can do to practise and experience **acceptance,** and train your **courage/willingness** and **acceptance muscles** at the same time. These will enable you to fully engage in experiences you might otherwise find too hard and be tempted to avoid.

Engaging in practical exercises is also essential in truly understanding key new ideas presented here that might run counter to what you have been told in the past. The leaning in exercise will train your ability to face your own monsters without too much interference from your judging mind. It will put you in a place where you can experience them directly, and gain the courage to make contact with your discomfort. Without evaluation, judgement, or avoidance, which will likely occur and get in the way.

> **Leaning in Exercise**
>
> (based on Eifert et al., 2005)
>
> In this exercise, you are practising to move away from 'thinking mode' when you are face to face with your internal monsters. In the past, this might have often led you down the path of avoidance, for example, avoidance through overthinking. Now you are going to do the opposite.
>
> Reading and 'learning' cognitively about these things won't get you the skills you need. For change to occur, you must actually do the exercises. In this exercise, you will build on the skills you learned doing the Diary of Reactive Habits in Chapter 4.
>
> So, let's get to it.

Firstly, make a list of the most feared situations you face in your sport. Moments that you know, from experience, have been challenging, or which you can predict will be emotionally difficult. Having a range of small to big challenges might be useful.

Then, pick one of your challenges and describe it in more detail using the Diary of Reactive Habits template from Chapter 4. In doing so, pay attention to your responses to this challenge; pay particular attention to the 'evaluations' your mind enters into. What does your mind say is the worst thing that could happen, and why is this so bad?

For example:

'I walk up to the penalty area in an important game. Hundreds of people and my teammates are watching. I am having thoughts about missing and letting everyone down, about how devastated I would be if this occurred. I feel my stomach crunching; I feel a bit wobbly in my legs.'

Next, from 0-10, rate the **Willingness** you have to face the monsters hidden in this story. If you imagine your Willingness to accept these fears was somewhere on a scale from 0 to 10, with 10 meaning 'absolutely willing to have these on board', then, if your score is anything less than '8', imagine you have a willingness dial to your disposal, and set it as high as you think you can.

Next, from your list, pick one challenge you can use for the imagery exercise below.

Just like with Chinese handcuffs, where you have to 'go in' (in order to get some space to move) when you face the passengers in your scenario, the aim is not to pull away, but to **lean in**.

This means to fully experience and completely allow all that comes up for you: bodily sensations, thoughts, and emotions.

You might feel your body get more energised, your heart beating, muscles tensing. You might notice your mind preparing an escape plan. But you just keep going, strengthening those muscles and habits of willingness and acceptance in the presence of your fears; keep moving in the direction you have chosen with all this hanging around.

Remember that none of this will kill or harm you, even if it feels like it. Or, in other words, remind yourself that thoughts are just thoughts; feelings just feelings. No more, no less. Open up to their presence.

It might also help to briefly recall where you are going, and why! This means to consciously reconnect for a moment with the underlying **purpose** of your endeavour, and its relationship to your values; what is meaningful for you.

1. Now, with the scenario you have chosen, do the following: find a quiet place and sit in a relaxed manner.

2. Close your eyes and imagine your chosen scenario as fully as you can. If it helps to experience this more, try to remember a specific situation when this last occurred.

3. If you can remember one, bring it back to your mind as clearly as you can: what

happened, who was there, what did you see, hear, smell? What did you notice in your body, what thoughts came up in this situation?

4. Whatever comes up, don't pull away from it, but acknowledge it, and open up to the experience. Allow any feelings that you might be aware of to be felt. Allow unwanted or disturbing thoughts, such as thoughts of failure, to come up.

5. Literally try to open up to everything you experience: your feelings, thoughts, and bodily sensations.

6. Pick one of your feelings or bodily sensations and attend to it more closely. Where in your body does it start, where does it end, what does it look like, and what shape does it have? Does it have a texture? A smell?

7. Even if your mind tells you that you've had enough, allow the experience. Willingly, let it just happen.

8. Let go of any struggle with it, just allow it to be there; stay with it. Relax into it for a while.

9. When you are ready, pick another area of discomfort that has been triggered in your body.

10. Go through 5-7 again.

11. Complete with 1–2 minutes of an ordinary mindfulness exercise.

In the beginning, you will ideally audio record this sequence; leave sufficient time at each step, and play it back to yourself with your eyes closed.

In Chapter 2, we discussed the role of language in building relationships between things and concepts. Many of our uniquely human struggles originated in the development of our language ability, which includes the ability to reflect, think ahead, remember, and worry about events which are not occurring in the present (or might never occur at all).

This ability to worry about what might happen in the future, or to remember past negative experiences, is helpful in many ways as it allows us to anticipate problems and do something about them. We can think of solutions and put them into action. This is good for dealing with situations where we can move and manipulate things; that is, the world outside our skin. It is different when it comes to dealing with emotional reactions. We can rarely think our way out of emotions, and strategies of control don't work in controlling emotions, or work intermittently at best.

In a way, all our troubles began when Prometheus stole fire, or Eve gave Adam the apple. These are two of the countless stories our ancestors in different cultures told about our transition to become language-enabled Homo sapiens.

Because this is when our struggles began, a little thought experiment might assist you in imagining how you could encounter internal discomfort in a different way. Pretend for a moment that Prometheus had never, metaphorically, stolen fire from the gods (i.e., we never developed language-based understanding). Imagine you were a wolf or lion on the hunt, or even an antelope running away from the hunter. For these animals, the signal that travels through their bodies would not arrive somewhere in a part of the brain that is prone to overthinking and 'not wanting' certain thoughts and feelings. They would simply respond in the best way possible, without undue interference from their minds. Try to imagine how this might translate into a sporting situation where you struggle with your internal discomfort? How would you respond to the situation, if you were not burdened with overthinking?

Certain bodily signals such as a beating heart, tense muscles, sweating, and extraordinary alertness would simply be a part of the overall experience. For the wolf, there is no need to label his experiences as 'bad' or 'good'. If you responded in a similar way, in the here and now, they would not lead to a thought like 'I am going to lose this game and then what?' They would not mean 'My friends won't respect me as much later'. These internal experiences are simply signals from your body that your skin is hot and wet, that your heart beats fast, your muscles are tense. That's all. Then your attention would go to the animal you are hunting – the game you are playing.

The Lean In exercise asks you to make mental images of your internal experiences. In order to do this, it suggests you go through all your senses and describe the physical experience you are having. This process achieves two things:

1. It brings your attention very much back to the original signal
2. It puts you into 'Observer mode'

Both of these enable you to become more flexible, and to respond to a situation more freely, without undue interference from the language processing part of your mind.

This exercise also asks you something else. It asks you to increase and develop the courage and willingness to experience unpleasant feelings, and thoughts; to imagine that you turn your 'willingness dial' up high.

Remember Eminem in the movie 8 Mile when he had to perform and was so nervous that he vomited and still performed? That is the type of courage we mean.

Conrad harnessing the Tiger Inside

We have now learned that Wayne's attempts to get rid of this inner discomfort are 'unworkable'. But there is also something else Wayne should know. Even if he could, it might not be such a good idea to get rid of all of the physical sensations inside his body in the first place! Some of these monsters, or passengers, are made of the stuff that he should be attending to, teaming up with, and using to his advantage.

Like the skilled sailor who harnesses the wind in a storm to their advantage, you can use the energy that you feel in your body during a competition to your advantage!

Imagine for a moment that an Olympic swimmer, basketball player, or other athlete could just turn that fear button off! Not the excitement, and not the adrenaline; just the fear. What would happen?

Also, if you focus too much on trying to relax before the whistle blows, you might lack the energy you need in order to run as fast as possible, jump as high as you can, and react quickly in the way you have practised, again and again as part of your training.

You have probably heard the term 'Fight and Flight response'.

'In essence, the right combination of cognitive, affective, and physiological conditions allows well-learned skills to occur in a seemingly effortless and automatic manner' (Gardner & Moore, 2007) – example: running

This biological response is usually explained by harking back to our caveman ancestors and the response they had when they faced a tiger. It pretty much explains why having this response was not only essential for your ancestors' survival, but is also necessary for yourself in a competition: your body responds in a way that is close to ideal for fighting and running.

If someone was to measure your indicators of physiological arousal, they would not find much difference between 'anxiety' and 'excitement' as states of arousal. But the meaning your mind attaches to each state makes all the difference to your experience.

> **Interpretation of arousal and performance**
>
> There is some hard, scientific evidence that supports this idea. Jones, Hanton and Swain (1994) found that athletes who interpret somatic arousal as 'helpful', maintain focus on the task at hand and perform well. Conversely, those who don't like it, often begin to focus on their inner processes instead of the task-relevant stimuli, which then interferes with their performance.

We would guess that in your chosen sport you probably need some fight or flight responses too! So why not embrace and harness them? Your body is doing exactly what it's meant to do here! What you might consider to be your old passengers – getting in the way – could possibly be part of a support team that's working on your side.

In a nutshell, not all that seems unpleasant is bad. In fact, it could be the opposite! Instead of fighting unpleasant experiences, **accept** what you can't change, and act **courageously** in what you need to do. Harness these sensations, and signs of your body's energy being stimulated, to perform even better.

This acceptance is a step that goes beyond tolerating things that are uncomfortable or challenging. We suggest you don't just passively accept, but that you actively invite these sensations in.

More easily said than done? Before your next competition, remind yourself of the reasons you engage in your sport. Be aware that this is a special time in your life that you might one day look back on with pride and enjoyment. Remember that this inner agitation you feel could possibly be useful. In short, focus on what you want and value, not on what you want to avoid. Focusing on this in the context of an important event might result in you feeling excited rather than anxious.

A time for calmness

There are many times in an athlete's sporting life when being overly excited is not very useful. There is a time and place for everything, and strong physiological arousal – whether due to anxiety or excitement – is not always helpful; such as when you are trying to sleep the night before your next competition. In situations where being calm and relaxed is useful, trying to control your anxiety might work for some people, some of the time. Others, though, might struggle in their use of traditional strategies to control their emotions, such as positive thinking or distraction.

Earlier on in this chapter, we explained why this might be difficult, and what usually happens when you try too hard to suppress certain thoughts or replace them with positive ones. So, what should you do when you actually want to lower your arousal levels the night before (or during a break in) your competition? The ability to relax and lower your heart rate at night would actually help your body to recover and gain new strength, allowing you to wake up refreshed. However, if you are lying in bed battling your thoughts, this is unlikely to happen.

The answer is not to battle.

Some of the exercises, further on, will help you to achieve this state, and the better you get at being aware of, and defusing from, your thoughts and feelings, the less entangled you will get with them. The more you practise, the better you will be able to do what counts in the moment. When you are in bed, what counts is relaxing. It helps to practise the skill of relaxing your body, in a mindful and calm way.

This might seem contradictory advice on one level. First, we tell you to accept the symptoms of anxiety; then we say learn to relax when it is the right time. However, looking more closely we are suggesting the same process. When you are in a competition and notice your anxieties, we suggest that you do this mindfully, in a calm way, and then direct your attention back to playing the game without spending effort and attention on controlling anxiety. Let's look at this more closely.

Mindfulness, Defusion, and Anxiety

The purpose of learning 'defusion-skills' and 'mindfulness' is primarily not to make you feel better, but to change how you relate to your inner experiences, or how you experience your thoughts and feelings. This change in 'relating' could be translated as you treating thoughts as not necessarily a reflection of 'truth', but as ideas your mind comes up with all the time.

Having thoughts is just one set of a variety of internal and external experiences. Realising that, and acting on it, means you give less primacy to thoughts, and rigid patterns of thinking and behaviour. In doing so, you free yourself to be present to all the relevant stimuli in your environment, and attend to those that matter most.

Let us explain this with an example.

If Wayne looks 'from' the position of his thoughts (as if they were fully accurate), he might walk up to the penalty spot with the thought 'I must not miss this shot, or everyone will blame me forever'. This thought then becomes akin to glasses he is wearing, which colour or shape how he views the world. So, he looks at the ball with trepidation, he glances at the faces of his teammates expecting to see doubt and uncertainty. Wayne's negative expectations make it much more likely that he will interpret nuances – which could mean three or four different things – as confirming his fears. He looks at the coach and interprets his expression as not expecting anything great. In this example, Wayne 'looking from his thoughts' leads to anxiety.

What would Conrad do? Conrad would notice a thought of doubt crossing his mind and would let it pass. He would not try to control his thoughts in the same way that he would not try to control rain clouds. He can then pay full attention to his hand gripping his tennis racket, to his feet standing in the correct position firmly on the ground, to the energy building in his body. This is Conrad **looking at** his thoughts as one of many experiences. This will help him to remain calm and not develop anxiety.

With exercises like the ones further on, we are aiming to help you develop a 'meta-level' sense of an observer self that is not too absorbed by the mind's constant chatter and its bodily responses. Instead, you will be able to develop a larger, more removed and complete view of your experience and what is happening in the present moment. With practice, you will be able to switch from a narrow focus, required some of the time, to having a more all-encompassing or meta view (Self as Context).

Please note that we are not suggesting that there is such a thing as an 'observer self', as a quantifiable object. The sense of an 'observer self' is something that might arise out of awareness (Hayes et al., 2001). This too is (on one level) another idea the human mind has come up with. However, if you develop the ability to 'observe' or 'switch into observer mode', this can be helpful and can become another skill that assists you in defusing from inner experiences.

'Observing', rather than 'buying into' your mind's chatter makes it much easier to develop a stance of **acceptance** towards your inner events; one where you are aware of them mindfully, without trying to control them. This allows you to make the best choice needed in any situation, which often helps you to come back to what you should be attending to. Paradoxically, this might sometimes calm you down, even though this is not what you are aiming for.

We suggest that you do not get too hung up wondering if there really is another 'Self', or what the 'Self' is. This is a deeply philosophical topic that could get us off track here. However, there are actually physiologically changes that happen in your brain when you practise the type of exercises we discuss further on, and this is very close to what we have said earlier about 'building a muscle' or a new 'ability' by training your brain.

> **Brain Imaging**
>
> In 2008, Davidson and Lutz reported on brain imaging studies on Buddhist Monks.
>
> They reported how these studies suggest that, by meditating for tens of thousands of hours, these monks had altered both the function and structure of their brains.
>
> It was also found that when meditating, multiple brain regions relevant to 'attention' were activated: brain regions implicated in monitoring (dorsolateral prefrontal cortex), engaging attention (visual cortex), and attentional

orienting (e.g., the superior frontal sulcus, the supplementary motor area, and the intraparietal sulcus).

An interesting finding was that expert meditators with many more hours of practice (44,000 in this example) than meditators with about half that amount showed less activation. This finding is similar to findings related to other skills such as language acquisition, and is believed to support the idea that after very extensive training, attentional focus can be sustained with minimal effort.

Studies with athletes, specifically, show one simple thing: if you practise – and become good at something – it becomes effortless. This means that your brain's resources can then be used for other relevant tasks during performance.

The Japanese researcher Eiichi Naito studied MRI images of the footballer Neymar's brain when dribbling the ball, and discovered that he showed only about 10 % of the brain activity that a more unskilled player would use doing the same task. He concluded that Neymar's brain was almost on 'autopilot' while handling the ball. Naito came to similar conclusions when comparing skilled and unskilled athletes in other disciplines such as swimming.

Two strategies Conrad woulduse

There are two types of practice Conrad would use that will help you to deal with uncomfortable thoughts and feelings.

1. Strategies to defuse things in the moment.
2. Strategies that build brain muscle, or attentional ability, for the long term.

A trained and more efficient brain will make it easier to lift your mental weights when you need to. You'll be aware where your mind's attention is going, and be better able to move it to where you want it. These skills are similar to any physical skill, and like learning a somersault, need practice to become ingrained.

Building flexible attention

The following practice is designed to help you build your ability to live with anxieties and pressure in a way that does not interfere with what you are about to do.

> **Building the Attention Muscle**
>
> The Leaf Exercise, further on, demonstrates how the mind typically works. It will help you to learn to pay attention.
>
> In this exercise, you are doing several things: you use the act of watching an imaginary stream as your 'anchor'. This is your FOCUS for the duration of this practice. This is the imaginary place you always go back to, if your mind wanders off.
>
> Don't worry. You are not Conrad in the heat of sporting competition. Nothing bad will happen if your mind wanders off. On the contrary, bringing your mind back to its focus is akin to the act of lifting a dumbbell. It builds the skill of noticing being caught up 'in' thoughts, and returning your

attention to the task at hand. If you notice your mind thinking about dinner tonight, gently bring it back to watching the stream, and voila – your brain muscle will have grown a few nanometres or grown a few more neural connections!

You may experience a whole lot of other stimuli that will take your attention away from your focus. Your mind may come up with random thoughts, you may experience feelings that relate to these thoughts, and there might be pain from just sitting still. That's all ok. It's perfectly normal. Instead of buying into all the internal and external stimuli, you will just notice them around you, and go back to watching the stream – detached and observant.

A script of the exercise is provided. Read and remember the instructions, or speak into your smartphone to record them, and then play this back to guide you through the exercise.

Exercise 1 – The Leaf Exercise

Close your eyes and imagine you are sitting in a nice setting in nature, with a small stream flowing in front of you. We would like you to watch this imaginary stream as it flows by.

On the stream, you see leaves that have fallen from the trees around you. Your task is just to watch the stream with the leaves floating by; keep it in your imagination.

Most people notice that, every now and then, their minds come up with various thoughts. These can be thoughts about important and unimportant things, like what you need to do this afternoon. Each time a thought pops up, make a mental image of that thought. Either a sentence or words (like in a cartoon thought bubble), or a more visual image like a picture.

Then imagine putting that thought on one of the leaves on the stream. You look at your thought and you watch it float along with the rest of the leaves. Then go back to watching the stream, the anchor of your attention. Keep doing this for a while... (leave a one-minute pause if recording this). Sometimes you will notice that you have been following a different train of thought for quite some time. It is great that you noticed.

You are getting practised at being aware of your mind's habit of running loose with random thoughts and taking you away from your focus. You make a mental image of the last thought you had, place it on a leaf, and let it float along the stream with the other leaves. Then simply go back to watching the stream… (pause for one minute or longer). Now, close the curtain on this scenario, take a deep breath, be aware of the world around you, open your eyes, and come back fully to where you are.

It might be a good idea to do this exercise at least two or three times a day. Start by doing it for a short length of time where you can concentrate fully (e.g., one or two minutes). As you get better at being present for most of this time, you might want to stretch this time out. Either mentally rehearse the exercise and put on a timer, or record it to your phone for a set number of minutes.

As always, practice is essential in order to develop your skills, and as we explained with the research about the meditating monks, plenty of practice quite literally helps to alter the brain structure in a way that makes it work more efficiently.

Some exercises could lend themselves to your ongoing regular practice; the leaf exercise or similar meditation or mindfulness practice included.

Summary

- Thoughts are not reality, and do not always require our action.

- Aim to notice random or fearful thoughts, and **refocus** on what action is important now.

- Fully notice thoughts and feelings, briefly, and come back to what you want to focus on (instead of fusing with them). In other words: enhance self-regulation of attention.

- In a challenging situation, be guided by your values and purpose when choosing a direction, not by the temptation to reduce unpleasant emotional experiences.

- If anything, welcome your experiences, especially when some of the things going on inside you can actually enhance your performance. You might even feel excited instead of anxious!

Chapter 6

Motivation, Willingness, and Commitment

As an athlete, you need to do a lot of things that 'normal' people would not consider to be ingredients for a good day: you might get up before sunrise, lift weights until it hurts, or push yourself up a mountain on your bike to the point of exhaustion while the wind howls and the rain hits your face. Your motivation and willingness to train, and your commitment to your sport, is probably what keeps you going.

For someone who observed you without knowing the context and the purpose of your endeavours, you might look like you are undergoing torturous activities comparable to a slave building the pyramids in ancient Egypt.

Yet, the experience you might be having is likely very different from forced labour. The difference is related to the reasons you are doing it: the 'why'. This 'why' lends a quality to your experience that is completely different.

In Chapter 3, you learned a lot about the 'why'. You learned how to identify your values more clearly, and how the things you do as an athlete are all expressions of these. However, this is not always as easy as it sounds. Hopefully, you are now fully aware of how anxiety can make it really difficult to get up and do what you ought to be doing.

But it is not just anxiety that can move you off course. We all have other passengers that can give us a hard time. The lazy passenger is one of them.

At times, she soothes you into turning over in bed one more time for a few more minutes of sleep, to hit the snooze button on your alarm instead of going out – into the rain – on a cold early morning. At other times, she reasons with you that you don't need to push yourself quite so hard in training because you are on top of your game already, or you had a very difficult day yesterday and need to take it easy now. This chapter is about how to deal with the lazy passenger.

Before we go into more detail on this, please take a baseline of your ability to hold your breath. This is an exercise in Willingness, and we will get back to this, and explain more, later on in this chapter.

> **Holding your breath**
>
> Get a timer, relax, take a deep breath and then hold it for as long as you can. Then make a note of the time you lasted. (based on Hayes & Smith, 2005) We will get back to this later.
>
> Note: Do not attempt this exercise if there is a medical reason not to. The authors and the publisher advise readers to take full responsibility for their safety, and to know their limits.

On some level, what we are going to suggest, here, will be very similar to what you have learned in the chapter on dealing with anxiety, and similar again to what follows in other chapters about the different kinds of barriers you might encounter. This is because, on a basic level, underlying principles for dealing with all the passengers are very similar.

When you hear your alarm ring in the morning, and it's cold, dark and windy outside, then you need to make a decision: do you get up, get dressed and go out to train? Or do you stay in bed? Or, in other words, do you do what is in line with what matters to you most (your values), and what will take you in the direction you want to go? Or do you do what's easy and rewarding in the short-term (although ultimately unsatisfying, and which sabotages your efforts to move toward those things you value)?

Short-term versus long-term? Who is in charge, the lazy passenger looking for the easy way out – or the driver steering the bus (you)?

In a way, this is similar to the decision you have to make when dealing with your anxious passenger. That passenger wants you to take it easy. Take a turn; do not walk up to this penalty spot. To feel less fear. As the driver of the bus, however, you want to move towards a direction that matters to you. If the part of you that wants to roll over and enjoy the warmth of your bed a bit longer is strong and persistent, then you need to know how to respond. This response, and what helps you to choose it, is in many ways similar to the response you learned when meeting your anxious passengers in Chapter 5.

We suggest you take note of this lazy passenger; acknowledge it, feel it, accept it is there, and keep steering your life-bus in the direction you are heading.

The willingness to suffer for what matters

It is not always being lazy that makes things harder for you. There is also the lack of willingness to suffer discomfort.

Like the guy who turns up for training and gives at least 70 %. But if his body hurts a lot, or he is really out of breath, then he is quite happy to let up; he's resigned to the idea that he's given all he can give and that more is just not possible today. You might think that he lacks commitment, but he also lacks the willingness to **experience discomfort** for his goals. Sometimes – when this is too hard to admit – he buys into the belief that 'more is not really possible', or the equally silly and unhelpful view that 'I need to feel more motivated before I can engage in this activity'.

Willingness is a key ingredient that will make you a driver who is in charge of your bus. In the same vein that acceptance and courage are essential for dealing with the anxious monsters, willingness and commitment to values are other key qualities we need when the going gets tough.

All of this requires self-awareness; the awareness to recognise and name the passengers that are coming up and urging you to change course. They can be very sneaky, and try to run things, hoping you won't notice.

Imagine you are biking up a mountain, and everything really hurts; your legs, your lungs, you are out of breath, and you feel fatigued. But the training plan you have set requires you to give close to 90 % of your maximum ability in this session. You could just stop there and then, you could tell the coach this was all you had; that your performance was close to 100 %. But who's speaking? You or your passenger?

What if the pain and fatigue you felt led your mind to suggest 'I can't do this any longer', and you didn't even notice? The 'Holding your breath exercise' which we are about to explore in more depth, can help you to become aware of inner experiences and fusion that occurs during a specific challenge that creates discomfort.

> **Accepting and Defusing discomfort.**
> **Holding your breath, the second time**
>
> In this exercise, we ask you to once again sit with a stopwatch and hold your breath for as long as you can. This time, however, we would like you to meet the discomfort you will encounter in a specific way: see if you can take an interested and slightly curious attitude to what you experience. Try being open to your experience; observe what happens as you hold your breath. Like a bus driver who listens, is curious, and clear about where she is heading while willing to have all of her passengers on board (the nagging ones and the lazy ones alike).
>
> So, this time, when you feel an urge to breathe, do any of the following. Sometimes focus on one at a time; at other times, you might hold more than one strategy in mind when meeting the urge to breathe.

- Notice where exactly in your body this urge to breathe sits. What is the feeling? Where does it start, and where does it end? If it has a shape, what is it? Is this near the surface of the skin, or deeper in the body? Is it hot or cold? Does the feeling move? What colour is it?

- Allow that urge to just sit there. Increase your willingness to have this experience to 8/10 on the willingness scale.

- Watch any feelings that you might notice. Name them, welcome them, and sit with them for a moment.

- Notice the thoughts your mind is producing, including sneaky thoughts that will urge you to take a breath just now. Thoughts like 'This will do. This is enough'. Listen to them.

- Notice what else is in the room around you; the other unrelated things you can hear, see, smell, feel. Also, notice other bodily sensations you experience at the same time.

The holding your breath exercise is a great way to practise your skills while creating strong discomfort. Here you are using mindfulness and defusion strategies, along with willingness and acceptance – while staying on your chosen path – for as long as you can.

How does this translate into 'real life'? Once again, imagine you are biking up that hill and giving close to your maximum effort. Once you have done a training drill like climbing up a hill a few times and observed yourself, you will be aware of all the physical sensations you experience; the subtle ways in which your passengers will try to give you justification to take it easier, and the ways in which you fuse with the reasons they give. So, next time you do this training run again, meet your passengers in a new way: just notice them, acknowledge them, feel the pain in your muscles, be slightly interested in what's going on in your body, and go back to the task you have set for yourself. In other words, do not let any of your passengers take the steering wheel. Or, this time, do not fuse with any of them. (note 1)

---

1. Obviously, do not ignore sharp or unusual pains which could indicate an injury, or medical need.

Let's consider the situation where you have committed to an early morning training session, and you just want to turn over and go back to sleep. How would you translate what you learned in the breathing exercise to this situation? You could notice what goes through your head; you might feel this urge in your body to enjoy the warmth of your bed a little longer, the desire to turn over and go back to sleep. This urge starts somewhere in your body, it ends somewhere, it will have a shape or area it covers, and certain sensations associated with it. Your task here is to observe this, feel it, and get up. Because getting up and doing the hard work reflects what matters to you most / the kind of person you want to be / the path you have chosen. Once you have been able to endure the strong discomfort of holding your breath, and responded in a defused manner, this response will become easier to switch into over time. You simply have to remember to bring these skills, and these responses, to similar situations. Like grunting out one more push up when your body is exhausted, or doing a final sprint at the end of a long training run.

Making Excuses

Our minds are very clever at tricking us into doing things that are not in our true interests, even though they might seem completely rational. The passenger we mentioned earlier in this chapter might come up with some good reasons why turning over in bed one more time is a perfectly valid idea. She might say, 'You are probably tired because you trained extra hard yesterday, you better have some more rest', or 'Well, you are ahead of the rest of the team anyway, just start training properly tomorrow and enjoy today'. She might remind you that you felt a bit under the weather yesterday and that without some extra rest you might catch a cold.

Likewise, when you are out running, trying to get to over 90 % of your anaerobic capacity, you might feel tempted by these other passengers we discussed. Passengers who provide you with very similar good 'reasons' for why you should maybe not work quite so hard. 'It's not your day today, don't be so tough on yourself', 'Who knows if that training schedule is all that it's made out to be anyway; so far you achieved everything at 80 %. You don't always need to be that perfect', or 'The coach is not paying that much attention today, take it easy'.

Sometimes these 'reasons' are so clever that we convince ourselves that we have made the better choice for our own good.

Now, let's say Sally comes up with a host of other 'reasons' for her uncommitted training performances. Imagine reasons like:

- 'I can't run that fast when I am tired.'
- 'I can't swim when it's that cold.'
- 'I did not feel motivated to get up at 5 am after a night of broken sleep.'
- 'There is no point in training when I am tired.'

How would you, as her teammate or coach, know if she is reason giving – making excuses to avoid her commitments – or if she is making rational choices?

ACT term: 'Reason Giving'

Earlier in this book, we talked about fusion with your thoughts. The more you fuse with a particular thought, the more influence it might have on your behaviours. Take any of the examples previously given; an individual who is highly fused with the thought 'It's ok to take a day off training when it's too cold outside' is more likely to actually skip the training session than an individual who is mindful of her thinking and treats 'thoughts as just thoughts', rather than causes or truths.

A thought cannot control or cause your behaviour, but it can influence it.

Reasons can only become problematic when we fuse with them, and see them as representing reality, rather than just one way to look at 'reality'. In our verbally dominated world, it has unfortunately become acceptable to give verbal reasons as explanations for behaviours. If someone says 'I felt too anxious to do xyz so I stayed at home', anxiety is often accepted as a

> cause for this behaviour rather than an emotion we chose to avoid. Thus, we have all learned to resort to verbal reason giving as a means to justify behaviours, even those that are not in line with our values and commitments.

It's simple. None of the reasons given previously would physically prevent Sally from doing what she has set out to do. All of them are Sally's mind engaging in reason giving.

What is a 'real' and 'good enough' reason then, you might ask? Here are two. 'I have a broken leg, I cannot run'; 'I twisted my ankle yesterday and it is still sore. I should take it easy today'.

While this might seem clear, maybe you are still not sure in what category some of the other 'reasons' your mind presents, fall into? Ask yourself this: if someone close to you was kidnapped, and your training action right now was the ransom – would you be able to do it? For example, could you train for one hour between 5 am and 6 am if this was required to get your loved one back? If you can, then any other rationale is 'reason giving'. There are exceptions, of course, in that you might do activities that are detrimental to your health; for example, train with an injury that does damage. This is not what we are talking about here and will be covered in more detail in Chapter 8, where we discuss 'Pain' and other passengers.

Uncoupling

When we are fused with our thoughts, we can quickly align our feelings and behaviour with random statements our mind might be making. 'It's too cold to train today' can become a feeling of dread and our corresponding (avoidance) behaviour can be to stay at home and watch the news instead. This might almost seem natural to us, especially when we are fused with other ideas like, 'I need to feel motivated before I can train properly'. The truth is, however, that we can do a whole lot of things even if we don't feel like it, or if our mind tells us we 'can't'. Want to try it out?

The following exercise will give you an experience of 'uncoupling' your behaviours from the content of your mind's stories (your thoughts).

Mini exercise: Independence Training

Sit in a chair. Then think repeatedly 'I cannot get up and walk around.' Try to even feel this statement in your whole body, a sense that you cannot get up!

Next, while repeating this, and really trying to feel it, get up anyway and walk around. For half a minute.

Keep repeating to yourself the thought 'I cannot walk around' while doing this. Try to keep the body feelings you had noticed in your awareness – while you do this – as well.

Then become aware of the discrepancy between the thought 'I cannot get up and walk around' and the action you are engaged in.

We know you may get the point of this exercise without doing it, and you might be inclined to keep reading instead of actually trying the exercise. We suggest that you do it anyway. The point of this exercise is not your intellectual understanding of this concept, but for you to experience this, and to get familiar with not automatically doing what your mind tells you. In this exercise, you are consciously experiencing the discord. In doing this, you can engage in a different level of learning.

To bring this point home, try the following exercise.

> **Mini exercise: Thoughts are just thoughts as a habit**
>
> For one week, 3-5 times a day, engage in an activity for the duration of one minute, while simultaneously telling yourself that 'I cannot do x', where x is your chosen activity. This could be brushing your teeth, tying your shoes, or walking. Anything at all.
>
> While doing this, be fully aware of the discrepancy of your mind's chatter and your action.
>
> You might set yourself random times (use an alarm) and continue what you are doing anyway while thinking you can't.

Advanced

Once you master the basic version of this exercise, step this up one notch.

Choose an activity that is slightly challenging for you and use some of the 'reason giving' your mind typically engages in for not doing it. For example, if you have had trouble getting up straight after your alarm rings, then get up straight away while telling yourself (for one minute) that 'It is too hard to get up this early, I can't do it.' If you bike up a hill and you know your mind will probably say 'Ease up now, it's getting too hard to keep going' then be alert to that moment, think the statement deliberately, and keep pushing for half a minute longer.

This exercise will give you practice in uncoupling, which is basically a form of defusing from your mind's chatter and reason giving, and can help you to become more alert to moments when you tend to fuse quickly (without awareness) with what your mind suggests.

Doing what needs to be done: freedom from thought

Now, you might think 'Ok, I get it, I can do something different to what a thought that I am having tells me. But what if I feel really intensely that I don't want to do, or cannot do, a specific activity?' You might think of getting this feeling after you resolved to jump off a 5 m diving board into the water, or decided to take an ice bath straight after waking up and getting out of bed. Before answering, we would like you to consider this: who told you that you have to feel motivated in order to act motivated? The I was not motivated enough reason is so common that it deserves special attention.

There seems to be a prevailing idea that people have to feel something in order to execute an action successfully. Quitting smoking, going to the gym – these are activities people often only start when they 'feel motivated'. As a result, people try reading motivational books, or listen to motivational speakers, in order to generate the feeling which they think they need before things can get started.

The good news is that feeling motivated is not required for you to make things happen. All that is required, is that you have chosen what you want to do, that you have made a roadmap that tells you what needs to be done next, and for you to then set out and do it... in the same way that the dishes just have to be done.

The issue is that many of us have accepted the idea that 'reasons' can be 'causes'. Statements such as 'I did not take this penalty because I felt anxious about looking stupid', or 'I argued with the ref because his decision was unfair' are widely accepted as describing rational cause-effect relationships. This, however, is yet another example of how our verbal abilities and language-derived thinking cloud our view of life. Verbal formulations, ideas, and feelings cannot be true causes of events.

(copyright Joseph Ciarrochi, used with permission)

When you consciously observe yourself in action, you might find that feeling motivated often results from action. You don't feel like going to training, but once you are there, you get into it. This is a very common experience. Engaging in meaningful activity will – more likely than not – give you a sense of 'feeling motivated'. 'Motivation' does not magically occur in a perfect moment; and we do not need to wait for it. It is not a requirement for action.

Feeling motivated might make it easier to act, and engaging in activity helps us to feel motivated. It works both ways. We only have control over one of these, though. Guess which one.

A useful concept in behavioural science is that of 'acting as if'. Often, athletes might not know where to start when they don't feel motivated to do something they aspire to. Wayne or Sally might think that first they 'should', or need to 'feel confident' or 'feel motivated', before they can do what's required. While we agree that it can be easier to act if you 'feel like it' already, there is a problem with waiting for this to occur. It is not something you can easily control; while 'just doing' something is completely in your control.

We understand that for many, this might be a difficult concept to translate into action if the task seems daunting! Preparing for a marathon run when you haven't trained in years, or getting up at 6 am and running for an hour in the rain can be a challenge. These are difficult things to do. In the following exercise, we describe a way of achieving this, one step at a time.

Acting as if – Getting a foot in the door

For this exercise, we assume you already have your long-term goals and short-term actions identified – based on your values worked out in Chapter 3.

Now, select the action you might struggle to execute and break it down further. Assume you had a plan to 'go jogging for 1-hour, starting at 6am' but you have failed to meet this goal numerous times. Now, break it down into smaller steps. Make the steps so small that you can muster some belief that you will do it; no matter how minuscule. If all you believe you are capable of, right now, is walking around the block, then just take that action. Do it. One step at a time. Make 'walking around the block' your minimum training plan for today.

More likely than not, this will give you some 'motivation' in the sense of a feeling or desire to engage in the activity. Importantly, it will also strengthen your belief that you can do something. You will more easily believe that you can probably

> do a bit more tomorrow. And you might, as a bonus, even feel a bit more motivated to run around the block twice. That's a start. And it is moving you in a direction that matters to you.

When engaging in an activity, a whole lot of passengers could come up to you and say things like 'This is pathetic, if I only walk around the block once I might as well stay in bed' or 'Look at you, the way you put on your shoes, just admit it, today you are not up for it. Let's start fresh tomorrow'. This is normal. This is some of your passengers playing up because they can sense that you are making a small step in a direction they don't like, and they are afraid you might do more. The way to deal with this is to keep going. Just do it; engage in your chosen activity and take your passengers for the ride, even if the ride is just a leisurely stroll around the block.

The Power of 'acting as if': Counter Clockwise

In one of the most famous experiments that used the 'act as if' principle, Ellen Langer (2009) got a group of men in their seventies and eighties to travel back in time by 'acting as if'. She randomly divided the men into two groups. The experimental group that was assigned to 'reliving the past' went to a centre full of items (e.g., black and white televisions that only showed old programmes), music, and reminders (e.g., photos, magazines) of a time 20 years earlier. Langer wanted to see how much this group, surrounded by reminders of a time when they were much younger, would act as if they actually were 20 years younger.

The second control group was told that the aim of this study was to find out about the effects of reminiscing about the past.

The effects for the first experimental group were dramatic. Within days, they were walking faster, many decided they did not need their walking sticks anymore, and more specific scientific measures showed improvements in memory, eyesight, hearing, blood pressure, manual dexterity and speed. While the participants of the control group also improved (that's why it is often called the 'placebo group'), the results of the experimental group were significantly larger. They also looked younger compared to the control group when impartial observers were judging their photos taken after their stay.

Acting as if does not end with you performing dreaded training drills only. You can extend the scope of this strategy by even acting as if you enjoy your training. Go all the way and experiment with Acting as if I enjoy X, where X is a drill you might dread, or execute with a sense of duty, rather than excitement or enjoyment.

For some, this might be lifting weights, for others swimming endless lengths in a pool.

These activities can be enjoyed! You can enjoy the simple sensation of cool air on your skin, the burning feeling in your muscles, and the sensations of your heart racing. Don't tell yourself you enjoy it, feel it. Engage in the process. This takes an attitude of mindful awareness and defusion or uncoupling from the thoughts and old automatic habits of thinking and feeling that might come up.

When you know that facing anxiety will make you a more courageous and present-minded athlete, this becomes easier to do. In a similar way, facing and welcoming one's 'difficult experiences and sensations' as a sign of your growth and commitment will change how you relate to, and think and feel about, your experiences. So, next time your muscles burn, rather than resenting them, bring joyous anticipation to proceedings!

Values and Motivation

It is important to remind yourself of your Why when engaging in tasks you struggle with, or want to avoid. Asking yourself the question 'Why am I putting myself through this?' and reconnecting with your underlying values can put things in perspective and give meaning and purpose to what would otherwise look like forced labour. While it might not always make you 'feel motivated', it will help to get things clear and to not fuse with the excuses and the 'reason giving' your passengers engage in. When these barriers to action come up, you will be in a much better position to deal with them; letting them tag along in the background while you get on with the business of living.

If, however, you keep struggling to do things, go back to the Values you identified earlier, and ask yourself which ones you are most willing to put in the effort for.

Doing what you love and loving what you do in every moment is not always the same. For example, you might think that you want to be an athlete; that this expresses some of how you want to live your life. However, this does not mean that everything you need to do (in order to be the type of athlete you aspire to be) is an enjoyable activity. If you are not willing to suffer for this Value, then you need to ask yourself if it is really that important to you. Or is it time to give it up so you can focus on something that might actually matter more to you?

Maybe you like the idea of being an athlete, but you don't like it enough to make it part of your life. What we mean is that many people like the idea of certain things they could do, have, or be. You can probably think of many people who would say 'yes' to the idea of having a big house, their dream car, the ideal partner, a perfect body, and yes, being a successful athlete. Who would not want some of these things? But that is not the question you need to ask yourself.

Are you prepared to do whatittakes?

The difference between those who want to be a great athlete and do what is needed, and those who don't do much about it, is not necessarily that the latter don't find the idea as appealing. The difference is – to a large degree – in how much they are prepared to do the hard work; how much they want to do the day-to-day activities involved in being a committed athlete.

Related to this is the concept of opportunity cost. Everything you want or do has an opportunity cost. That means, there is a price tag attached to it. The hard work you need to put in; the time spent on training that you cannot spend on other things. The money handed over for a car that cannot be spent on something else, like a holiday. So, ask yourself if you are willing to have all the difficult experiences, not just the glory and fun. Your willingness to bearing the opportunity cost of putting in the necessary time and effort, to be the athlete you want to be, is an important indicator of how much you really want it.

When you ask yourself this question, don't just imagine a fantasy of a gold medal hanging around your neck and fans cheering! Think about whether you are willing to commit to the early hours, the physical discomfort and pain, disappointments, frustrations, and the time spent in the gym working hard while you could be doing other things you might enjoy. What is your answer to this question? Or, in other words: can you love and commit to the journey and not worry and focus too much on the destination?

Two sides of the coin

You can think of living your value-driven life, and experiencing the discomfort, as two sides of the same coin.

On the one side, you have your most important value. For example, to keep learning and improving your skills in a chosen field, being competitive, a supportive teammate, being someone who keeps challenging herself.

On the other side of the coin, there is the cost involved in taking a path in line with your values: the pain, the foregone opportunities to hang out with your friends and drink, the potentially boring and repetitive routines your sport requires, like long hours swimming lane after lane while others are still in bed or enjoying breakfast in the café. There is also the disappointment when competitions don't go well, or you make mistakes, and all the difficult feelings and thoughts this might bring up for you.

There are two sides to everything we value; and the more important something is to us, the more we value it, the more intense our feelings associated with this value might become. The more you care about one thing in life, the bigger the potential for suffering on the other side of your coin! This is something many of us experience in relationships. When we really love a partner or a child, we are open to potentially disastrous negative feelings: feelings of loss, rejection, extreme sadness. Many find it difficult to fully commit to another person due to fusion with their fears of what might occur.

'Where there is love, there is pain' – Spanish Proverb

There are two sides to most situations which intrinsically belong together. The only way to avoid potential pain, suffering, and disappointment is to avoid those paths that lead to possible joy, friendship, adventure, accomplishment, and love. You generally cannot have one side without the other. That's life, and this includes everything you do in your sporting life.

> **Two sides of a coin exercise**
>
> 1. Think of all the values related to your sporting life. Take out a piece of cardboard (the size of a credit card), and write down (on one side) what matters most to you about this area of your life. Some examples might be: to strive, to be a supportive teammate. Use some one-word descriptors that summarise the essence of the athlete you want to be: a love of learning, to be courageous, energetic...
>
> 2. Now turn over the card. On this side, write down all the difficult experiences that you might have when you take action towards your values. This can include things like fear of disappointment, laziness, fear of letting down others, pain (emotional and physical). You might want to consider some of the

things you identified in earlier exercises, including bodily sensations, emotions, and negative thoughts you might get fused with.

3. Now take this card, put it in your handbag, pocket, bag, or wallet and for the next few weeks take it out several times every day; look at both sides of it and ask yourself: do I really want this? Do I fully want what is on this card, on both sides? Do I want to commit to this?

You can choose your values, you can choose your path, but you can't choose to have only one side of a coin. You can just want the result, but you get everything that's involved in the process of walking the path towards those results: monsters, flowers, and unicorns.

Reducing Passenger Opportunities

We pointed out, earlier, that you can't really kick the passengers off your bus; they are a part of the bus and of who you are (in the same way that a coin has two sides). But what you can do is reduce the opportunities for them to complain while you keep moving in the right direction.

What does this look like in practical terms?

There is a difference between you committing to fitness training every day (with your chosen gym being a 45-minute drive away), or you having a nice set up of basic exercise equipment in your backyard. The latter reduces the amount of effort (and opportunity cost) and thus the chances for your passengers to ask you not to exercise altogether. In the same vein, having your sports gear ready, next to your bed, or packed and in your bag, and unhealthy food somewhere in your garage on a faraway shelf (for very special occasions) all increase the likelihood of you making choices towards fitness and health.

Focus on process, not out come

If we continue with the bus metaphor, a happy driver is one who enjoys her trip as she travels in a meaningful direction. A driver who desperately tries to get to the next landmark or mile marker might experience much less enjoyment and reward. With less enjoyment and reward, there is less impetus and less strength to handle the difficulties that come along. What we learn, in applying ACT, is fully in line with the old saying that life is about the journey, not the destination. Or, in other words, the process of living rather than the milestones to be reached.

There is a story that demonstrates this (Hayes, Strosahl, & Wilson, 1999). Imagine someone who loves skiing and finds it fulfilling. She has chosen 'skiing' as what she wants to do and relishes her time in the mountains. One day, she takes the gondola to the mountaintop, puts her skis on, but before she can start her run, a helicopter lands near her. The pilot asks where she wants to go. She says she'd enjoy taking the run down the left-hand side of the mountain to the hut in the distance. Before she can refuse, the pilot pulls her into the helicopter and flies her down. Why not? He was going there anyway, and it's much faster. After a quick look around, he asks her what her plans are next. She points to another faraway hut. Eager to please, the pilot sits her down and flies her to the next destination. And the next and the next.

At the end of the day, our friend – who wanted to enjoy a day of skiing – had reached all her planned destinations, but enjoyed very little skiing.

This metaphor points out that often – in life – process matters over outcome. So, how can we enjoy the process more than we often seem to do? It would be a very difficult journey, and not a great time as an athlete, if every training session felt like a tedious chore. So, what can you do?

Instead of focussing on a faraway outcome (e.g., winning a race, making a certain time), focus on the enjoyable aspects and immediate rewards of the activities you need to perform along the way: connecting with your teammates, learning from your coach, the energy and sense of satisfaction from a training session done well.

The skier who has her eyes set only on the hut in the distance misses a lot of the skiing! If she has chosen a hut that is hours away, she might even feel slightly dissatisfied about the time it takes to get there. For the 'outcome-oriented mindset', the discrepancy between the distant goal and the current situation can become a source of constant dissatisfaction. Once the outcome is achieved, if ever, the sense of satisfaction is unlikely to last long. The outcome-oriented mind will quickly choose another goal and another sense of deficit will emerge, until this goal is reached as well. What you get is an imagined life that finds fulfilment somewhere in a distant future.

Conrad, on the other hand, will enjoy the small steps he takes in his training. The training itself becomes a satisfying practice of discipline and focus. Like the skiing, where taking turns and feeling the sense of movement in your body, and the cool air on your skin, can easily provide a sense of reward and satisfaction in the here and now.

Summary

- The often tedious, difficult, and painful tasks you do in training, can be accepted more easily if the Why (that is, your values related to these activities), are understood.

- Many of the responses you learned in the last chapter on dealing with anxious passengers can also be applied to the lazy passenger.

- Other aspects of responses you might have, include the willingness to experience discomfort and commitment to your values.

- It would be unhelpful for you to wait until you feel motivated before you engage in difficult activities, because this is not something you are likely to have direct control over. What you do have control over is your behaviour. So, if nothing else works, act as if you are motivated.

- Thoughts are not reasons. The reasons our mind gives us for not doing difficult activities can only become problematic when we fuse with them. Not training 'because you did not feel motivated' is only problematic if we accept reasons as causes. Thoughts, however, cannot cause you to do (or not do) something unless you allow them.

- It is important to be clear about your values, and to accept that each value-driven activity comes with opportunity costs. You need to be clear that you do not just like certain outcomes you wish to occur one day (e.g., a gold medal), but that you actually value the life of an athlete and all that comes with it.

- Practical arrangements like a packed training bag next to your bed might reduce the chance for difficult passengers to take over your steering wheel.

Chapter 7

Self – Esteem, Self – Concept and the Tyranny of 'Me'

If you have been practicing the mindfulness of breath exercise that we suggested in Chapter 2, you will probably have noticed that most of your thinking is all about you. It references you, or your relationship to other people and to things in some way: how you feel, what you are going to do, what you have done, or how things have impacted upon you. In other words, it's all about 'me', 'me', 'me'.

This is normal. It is how thinking works.

It is also the basis of how we see ourselves. We define and judge ourselves mainly through our perceived relations to others, and our attitudes towards things and events, our likes and dislikes. This defines our concept of self – the ideas we have about who we are, and what we are like. These ideas are generally simply automatic assumptions, and they go unquestioned. They just seem to be the way things are. In ACT terms, this is referred to as the conceptualised self. The unquestioned assumptions we make about ourselves.

This constant self-referencing along with our comparisons to others, and our ideas about how they see us, determines our self-esteem.

In this chapter, we are going to look at the problems associated with being fused with, or identifying strongly with, the conceptualised self, which in turn determines our self-esteem.

The Downside of Self – Esteem: I can vers us I feel

Self-esteem is a term most people are familiar with. It is generally seen as our sense of self-worth, or value. Unfortunately, there is often some confusion between 'self-efficacy' and 'self-esteem'.

Self-efficacy is the belief in your ability to perform or complete a task. It is related to concrete actions. Self-esteem is how you feel and think about yourself. It is an emotional response, but also involves self-appraisal, and comparisons not only with others, but with our expectations of ourselves. It is important to be aware of the difference between a sense of self-worth/esteem, and self-efficacy.

The common view is that without what psychologists have referred to as 'high' self-esteem, we feel useless, lacking in value, and, well, like losers. In the past, this has been fostered in sporting circles by the assumption that we not only need to believe in our ability to achieve (self-efficacy), but that it is necessary to think positively and tell ourselves, repeatedly, that we are winners, and that we will win, that we are special or talented, or better than the opposition. This is not self-esteem, but an attempt to artificially generate self-efficacy. Self-talk like this can be useful, but for many people positive thinking feels false and can backfire. One of the reasons for this is that, for many athletes, their self-worth is tied to the achievement of goals. This can be winning certain matches, getting into a specific team, running under a particular time, and so on. This is tying self-esteem to specific goals, rather than to valued ways of being. Values involve actions toward much broader aims, such as being a good friend, supporting the team, or always giving your best.

Managing or working with self-esteem is a tricky area to navigate as, of course, we need to believe in our ability to achieve (self-efficacy), and the desire to achieve does result in negative feelings of failure when we perform poorly. Failure to meet our goals is often accompanied by negative evaluations of our performance. This is useful as it can show us where we can improve and serves as a source of motivation (although it is somewhat negative). Where it is unhelpful, is if we allow failure to determine how we feel about ourselves in general, or beyond a relatively brief period following our poor performance.

As many sports people tend to tie their self-esteem to their achievement, it is affected by transient failures, and can lead to self-doubt, and prolonged periods of negative emotions such as anger and sadness which can be accompanied by negative self-evaluations or put downs. This tie to self-esteem can lead to fear of failure which impacts on subsequent performances, and to a lowering of self-efficacy. That is, we start to question our ability. The aim here, as in much of the rest of this book, is to learn how to defuse from fixed ideas about the self (self-esteem) when necessary and focus on self-efficacy, and on the task at hand.

Fear of failure

Many people are driven to perform by fear of failure. At some level, they feel they are 'not good enough' and may use sports to feel better, and to avoid feeling bad about themselves.

In many ways, using sport and activity to feel good is fine. It is a healthy, pro-social, expression of physicality and ability. Problems arise when sport, or achievement is too closely tied to our self-esteem and sense of self. This leads to fears of poor performance, looking bad, or making mistakes which, in turn, impact negatively on our performance. This happens by inhibiting our behaviour, putting an emotional block between what we have learned in training and its execution.

Fear of failure is also a poor motivational technique as involvement in sports becomes a way of avoiding negative feelings rather than chasing the positive. Training and competition can become a negative experience to be endured rather than something we do that is driven by desire and our values.

LACK OF COMMITMENT AND EFFORT

Fear of failure, or the innate desire to avoid negative feelings triggered by poor performance or errors, can lead to lack of commitment and effort.

If we don't really try – in training or in competition – we can protect our self-esteem by telling ourselves a comforting story. We can say to ourselves: it would have been different if we were really committed. We can imagine Wayne doing this, and we may have done it ourselves. One example might be slacking off during a match when things aren't going well, or when we are losing. Anyone who has seen a football team 'fold' once they are down will have seen when players aren't giving their best.

BLAMING OTHERS

If we blame others, then it is not our fault. That means that we don't have to take full responsibility for our performance and the steps needed to improve. This can lead to a lack of development and improvement.

In a team environment, blaming others can have toxic effects on the team. It creates distrust among team members, and increases anger, tension, and fear of failure for, at least some, team members. It also takes attention away from ways of dealing with the problem as responsibility is laid totally at the feet of others.

FEELING LIKE A FRAUD

Some athletes, no matter how accomplished, just don't fully enjoy their successes. Their deep-seated belief is that they are somehow flawed, or not good enough. They are fused with low self-esteem; the idea they are unworthy. Naturally, an emotional impact is attached to this belief. Taking pride in and celebrating their accomplishments triggers the flip side of high self-esteem. The 'I'm not good enough' feeling for some people.

The problem, like many we have discussed previously, is not low self-esteem, but,

1. believing the thoughts associated with this old programming

2. trying to avoid the feelings associated with them.

Feeling like a fraud can drive the other problems mentioned earlier: fear of failure, lack of commitment, and blaming others.

Wayne has gone for a Karate grading and failed. He did not get promoted to the next belt. He feels angry and ashamed in front of others at the Karate club, and goes home after the grading in a bad mood. On the way home, he is grumpy and a bit rude to his wife. That evening, she tries to reassure him and make him feel better, but he gets angry and blames her for his performance. If she didn't make such a 'big deal' out of him training so much he would have been better prepared. And if she didn't make him go out with friends last weekend, and stay up late during the week before the grading watching her favourite programmes, then he would have done better. Not surprisingly, they have an argument.

Wayne feels bad about his performance. His self-esteem has been damaged, and basically, he feels bad. His reaction is to blame someone else as a way of protecting his self-esteem. It is a way of convincing himself that the performance was not his fault. The purpose of blaming is to get rid of some of the pain and discomfort he feels. It doesn't matter who, or what, he blames – his wife, a training partner, or the Sensei.

Conrad has the same experience. He failed the grading. He is disappointed, and feels ashamed and a little angry at himself. What is different is that his self-esteem is less tied to his performance. While he is affected by failing the grading, and it hurts, his innate sense of himself is not really threatened. It is only bruised.

Conrad hurts, Wayne suffers. Pain + resistance = suffering.

Wayne resists and tries to avoid his negative experiences. Conrad accepts, defuses from suffering, and moves towards what he values.

This means that Conrad's behaviour is more open and responsive to the situation. This allows him to see it from the Sensei's point of view. Why did he fail? What did he do wrong? Was the problem with his physical preparation, his endurance, or was it with his technique? Maybe they failed him because he didn't attend enough classes? The difference is that Conrad begins to analyse what went wrong, and what he can do to rectify it for next time. He begins to see areas he can work on, and to develop a training plan to work on his weaknesses.

He also reacts differently to those around him. He is quiet on the way home, and while not in a good mood he doesn't take his disappointment out on others. He tries to relax that evening with his family and starts to feel better because he has the beginning of a plan to improve his performance.

The problems outlined come up due to our over-identification with our ideas about ourselves; namely, who we should be, and what other people might think of us. In other words, 'fusion' with a self-concept.

This applies to both high and low self-esteem. Those with a very strong identification with positive self-esteem can certainly lack commitment and effort in training and competition, at times, due to their innate sense of superiority. They also have a tendency to blame others for failures, and to protect their self-esteem if it is attacked or threatened.

Fortunately, we don't need to get rid of self-esteem altogether to perform well; feeling proud or satisfied after a good outcome, a team win, or a good performance, can be motivating, and pleasurable. There is certainly nothing wrong with feeling good about yourself now and then, or about acknowledging your faults so you can work on them. In terms of our overall view of ourselves, our self-concept, or self-esteem, it is important not to indulge these ideas about ourselves to the extent that they interfere with our performance. That is, not to tie or fuse our sense of self-worth strongly to our performance.

There are some things we can do to loosen the potential interference of self-esteem during competition or training. These methods build on the exercises you completed in previous chapters. The mere fact of becoming aware of our thoughts, our habitual emotional reactions to them, and to varying situations, is a big step towards being less susceptible to blows to self-esteem.

If you have completed the previous exercises, you have a firm foundation to work from. Before we get into the exercises themselves, we will outline one interesting study conducted using the Stress Inoculation Technique (SIT) developed by the psychologist Donald Meichenbaum. This technique has been applied in a wide range of sports settings with the result of reduced stress, and improved performance. While we will not be using this technique as it was originally developed, there are strong similarities to our approach. We believe it is a good example of the power of exposure in sports settings, and a brief description of the study will give you an idea of where we are heading.

In a study conducted with University level runners, one group were trained in SIT, and the other given simple relaxation exercises. This training took place over several sessions and the SIT group were trained to become aware of their thoughts, trained how to relax, and then instructed to imagine several situations.

The runners were primarily track athletes, so they were instructed to imagine various situations in competition – such as performing poorly, or having an injury – then noticing how they felt and returning to using their relaxation technique. Eventually, they imagined even more difficult situations, such as falling in a race, or causing other runners to fall, all while their family and others important to them were watching from the stands. And, once again returning to their relaxation strategy.

The runners' physical training remained unchanged from that of the rest of the squad.

The results were remarkable. For the SIT group, measures of aerobic capacity improved more than for their teammates who had the same training (as per the usual regime). They also showed a greater improvement in performance over the course of the season. All as a result of using their imagination in a controlled manner. This is a pretty impressive outcome.

From a psychological perspective, that intervention was basically an exercise in exposure. Exposure involves practice in experiencing unwanted thoughts, feelings, and reactions. This reduces their impact when similar things occur in the ordinary course of events. In ACT terms, this is also exposure to threats to our self-esteem or self-concept. We will use the abilities you have developed in increasing awareness of your body, your emotional reactions, and your thoughts, to make this as realistic as possible, with the aim of learning to defuse from perceived threats to self-worth. This defusion reduces the impact of threats to self-esteem in action.

You can see that, in some ways, it is very similar to what we have been doing in previous chapters using the Diary of Reactive Habits exercises. What we will do now is to build on those exercises.

The Walk – Through Exercise – Part One

For this exercise, we want you to think of some situations related to your sporting activity where you have felt shy, embarrassed, or as if someone is criticising you. These can be situations that have happened, or things that you fear happening. It can also be helpful to think of times where you have demonstrated some of the behaviour we have outlined above: fear of failure, lack of commitment, blaming others, or feeling like a fraud. We are looking for instances where you may have felt some threat to your self-esteem or self-concept.

Please write these down.

Think broadly and write down as many instances as you can.

Once you have done that, rate the examples according to how bad you felt at the time. With ten being the most intense and 1 being virtually no feeling at all. Then, put a star beside the examples that occur the most often. A short list might look something like this.

6	Stepping up to the golf tee with three people from another club watching.
10	Being corrected by my coach in front of the team.*
4	Missing a tackle.
10	Playing badly and being subbed.
8	Being heckled by a spectator.*
1	Getting undressed in the dressing room.*
3	Running past groups of people on a training run.*

What we are going to do is pick some situations to work on. We will do this by re-living the situations. In your imagination, we want you to 'walk through' a stressful or uncomfortable situation; starting from before it even begins. As we do this, it is important to attend to all of the things that come up for you. This includes bodily sensations, emotions, and thoughts; anything you become aware of. The aim is not to get to the end of the exercise, but to fully experience your reactions as you move through it.

Some people find it easier to start with something that doesn't bring up very strong feelings, and then work up to the very difficult experiences. This is a good way to approach this exercise if you have some situations that cause very intense reactions. However, it is important to start with something that is actually difficult, or uncomfortable for you. Don't pick something too easy. If you do, the situation you are imagining might not bring up strong enough feelings for you to be aware of them, or to get any benefit out of working with them. It is a bit like any training; you need to work near your edge, not well below it.

A good place to start is with situations of at least medium level intensity. It is also fine to start with really difficult situations. The important thing is not to rush through the exercises, and not to try to get to the 'end'. When we work with individuals we often don't even get to the 'end' of a chosen scenario; the part where – in real life – the situation would be over. The important thing is re-living your reactions to the situation. Not making it better, or making those reactions go away.

We will run through the steps of how to do the exercise, then give you an example to see how it might work (in practice) if we were sitting in the room with you. Briefly, you will recall a situation in your imagination, and relive it in as much detail as possible.

The Walk-Through Exercise

1. Pick the situation you are going to walk-through in your imagination.

2. Sit upright, relax slightly, then do several minutes of mindfulness of breath. Simply focus on the bodily sensations of breathing. Don't rush this part of the exercise but keep to five minutes or less.

3. Bring to mind the situation you want to work with, but start a few steps before the situation itself. (We will give an example on how to do this further on.)

4. Mentally walk-through events leading to the situation. Do this slowly. You might start by thinking about getting ready to leave home: collecting your gear, how you will travel to your destination, etc; thoughts you might be having about what will happen in the situation.

5. When doing this, in your imagination, be aware of what you are feeling. Are there any changes in your body? Do any emotions come up? What goes through your head? Be aware of

these. Then, recall your surroundings from that situation. Where were you? What could you see, and hear? You can use your experience of using the Diary of Reactive Habits as a guide for this exercise. Then go back to your mindfulness of breath. Stay with that for a few moments. Then go back to the start and mentally walk-through the process again.

6. Break the situation into brief sections like this and go through them slowly. In this exercise, treat thinking of the events – whether real or imagined – as a film and you keep rewinding back a scene or two. If you are not feeling strong emotions, or a lot of distress, then move the film on a bit farther. The point is not to get to the end of the film, or to the point where negative feelings are strongest, or to train yourself to feel nothing. The aim is to experience – as fully as possible – the emotions, bodily sensations, and thoughts that come up as you relive the situation in detail.

   As a guide to help you structure this exercise, you can label the intensity of what you feel (with 10 being extreme and 1 being hardly anything), and choose to move to the next part of the experience when the level of discomfort you feel on recalling the events in detail has reduced slightly from the strongest it ever was. As an example, if 10 was the most distress or worry you ever felt during a particular part of the walk-through exercise, (or the real life equivalent), move on when it is 7 or 8. If it was 6 or 7 at its strongest, move on when it is 5.

In your walk-through, you might not even get out of the house. Remember, the aim of the exercise is to re-live the experience in imagination, and to experience it as fully as possible.

We will use the first situation listed beforehand as an example. It is a composite of several real situations that have occurred with clients; we have combined elements from several people and changed things slightly, so they don't represent any one real person.

EXAMPLE

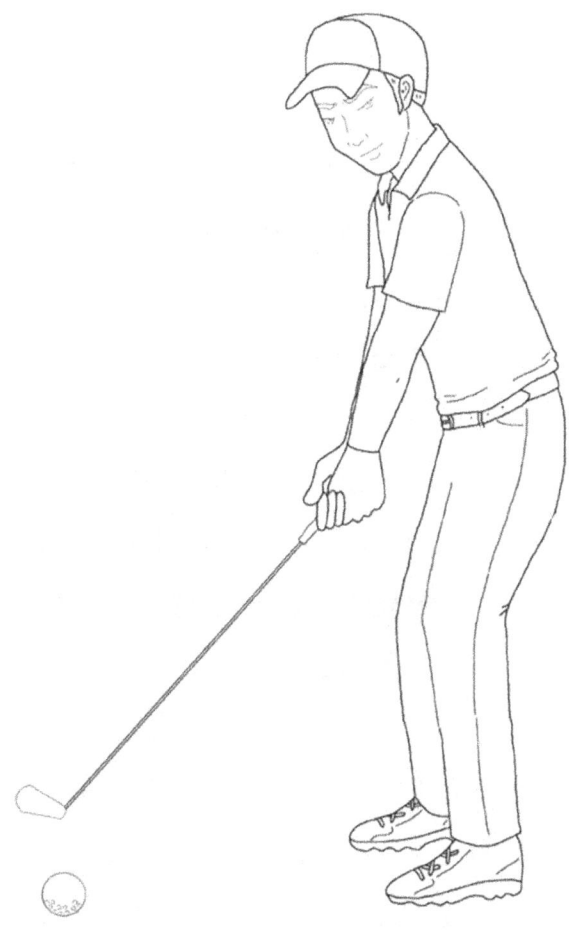

Conrad is an accomplished golfer who plays well when he is on his own, or playing with a few close friends. However, even in club competitions he plays much more poorly. He gets nervous about his performance, and he knows this is a problem, so he gets worried about it happening before it even starts. As a way of working with his anxiety in competition, Conrad used the 'walk-through' exercise.

In his practice, he started by doing five minutes of mindfulness practice (timed on his phone). Then he imagined the night before the competition (you can use a past event like Conrad, or something coming up in the future). He was in the kitchen making dinner and thought about getting an early night so he would feel good the next day. He imagined the kitchen, his stove, and sink, the lino, remembered the thoughts about getting to bed early, and a sort of sick jolt in his stomach. He described it as a sinking feeling, but also as shooting up towards his chest and throat. Conrad rated the strength of this – how distressing or unwanted it was – as around an 8.

Just like when using the Diary of Reactive Habits, Conrad noticed where the feeling was sitting in his body, and tried to be aware of its physical sensations (hot/cold, sharp/dull, moving/fixed, heavy/light, deep/near the surface). He opened his awareness up to any emotions he was feeling (a little scared and annoyed), and feelings in other parts of his body, his reactions (tension in the shoulders, clenching his jaw). Feeling these sensations briefly, he then took one deep breath, and rewound back to just before he started to make dinner. He imagined sitting at home in the lounge, what it looked like, attended to his breathing for 30 seconds or so, and started the walk-through again.

Conrad walked through his experience in the kitchen several times, then back to the start of the scenario. Each time, he was aware of the reactions in his body. When his distress got to 6, Conrad moved the scene on to later that evening, when he was lying in bed thinking about the competition, and about how he would freeze and make mistakes. He noticed his reactions, the feelings in his body, then mentally walked back to an earlier point in the evening when he was watching TV after dinner (you don't need to return your original starting point every time, just take a few steps back). Conrad got as far as imagining himself driving to the golf club, gripping the steering wheel, breathing shallowly, feeling a tightness in his stomach.

In this example of practice, Conrad didn't progress the walk-through all the way to the competition itself. That is not the point (although he could eventually, if he found it useful). The important thing is that he was practicing being fully open to, aware of, and engaged with, his experiences without adding anything extra to them or avoiding and fighting them. This means that he was learning how to defuse from his thoughts and perceived threats to his self-esteem. He was fully attending to the present moment and accepting his experience as it was. Not wasting time and resources on wishing it was something different. These are important skills when engaged in competition. Conrad was also taking committed action in line with his values. He was devoting time to an exercise that was not inherently enjoyable with a view to developing his abilities as a golfer.

This is a very valuable exercise. With practice, we can develop the ability to be less affected by threats to our self-concept. As a result, we can be more open to others, and to the situations we find ourselves in, reacting appropriately without the unnecessary filter of worrying about how we look, or how we will be seen by others, or ourselves.

The Walk – Through Exercise – Part Two

Another way our self-esteem is threatened is by our subtle expectations about how we should perform. We often have high, but vague expectations about ourselves, and what we should be able to do.

We want to be perfect.

We want to play the perfect game, run the fastest time, and win the biggest trophy. Most of us know, intellectually, that this is impossible, but it doesn't stop us from being fused with the idea that we should be more skilful, and more successful than we are.

Of course, wanting to improve and striving to perfect your skills is a good thing. If they don't negatively impact on performance. Fusion with an ideal self, or an ideal performance, means that we will generally disappoint ourselves. This fusion can lead to all the problems associated with attachment to self-esteem listed previously. It is also problematic as we are generally unaware of it.

It is unspoken, and is more of a feeling, or a pre-conscious process, than something we talk about or put into words.

It is important to remember that having an ideal and striving for perfection is very different from being fused with these expectations. Fusion leads to negative emotional reactions and takes energy and attention away from what we are actually doing in training or in competition. What we are aiming for is to foster the active pursuit of valued goals, driven by desire, while lessening the negative impact of reactions due to fusion with irrelevant expectations. Dreaming big is wonderful. As long as it is a specific valued dream, and not a series of vague unrealistic expectations we are fused with.

We work with these subtle expectations in the first part of this exercise. Because these expectations are subtle, and unspoken, you will probably have to make things up, rather than using a lot of personal experience. We start by imagining things turning out fine, with normally good results. Then, we imagine things being a bit better, then better, then better and better, to the extent that they are totally ridiculous. In Conrad's case the scenarios might be:

1. Goes to the match and doesn't make too many mistakes. Performs ok.

2. Performs better than usual. Lowest round in competition for several years. Complimented by friends, and club members.

3. Lowest round in competition ever. Gets compliments from opposition.

4. Best round ever. Wins club championship.

5. Asked to play pro-am.

6. Wins a Masters.

7. Buys a mansion in Hawaii.

You can see where this is going. It starts out with reasonable expectations, then moves to things that are, for most people, ridiculous. The aim here is to defuse from our unspoken expectations. To defuse from that part of our self-esteem that sees us as the centre of the universe and wants, wants, wants.

We are not suggesting wanting is wrong. Desire, wanting to do well, to achieve, and simply wanting to win, can certainly serve as an aid to performance. What we are defusing from in this exercise is expectation, and the negative effects of having those expectations thwarted. We are defusing from the thoughts, emotional reactions, and behavioural responses to those reactions that can form a filter between us and what needs to be done. That is, attachments and reactions that impede our performance. Such defusion aids simple attention to the task at hand, and allows our training to take over.

Go through this exercise just as in part one, slowly, carefully attending to whatever comes up as you imagine each situation: your bodily sensations, emotions, and thoughts.

Things to practise

The Walk-Through Exercise seems simple but is extremely powerful. It is worth spending time with it and working with both parts, dealing with feared or unpleasant situations, and with subtle positive expectations. It is also a very useful exercise for dealing with anxiety and with any difficult situations where you want to act in line with your values, and not simply react emotionally.

Summary

The things we covered in this chapter can be broken down to some simple ideas:

- It is useful to be aware of the difference between self-efficacy and self-esteem.

- Self-efficacy is belief in our ability to achieve and complete tasks.

- Self-esteem is how we feel, based on ideas and beliefs about our self-worth.

- While ideas about ourselves feel true, they are not always accurate or based on reality.

- High self-esteem is not always a good thing.

- Attempts to protect your self-esteem can lead to aversive control of behaviour, and to fear of failure, lack of commitment, and blaming others.

- Using the Walk Through Exercise helps us defuse from our fears, and our need to protect self-esteem. It exposes us to unwanted emotions and thoughts so they lose their hold over us.

- This allows us to chase our goals without the interference of unnecessary negative emotions. That is, it helps us focus and keeps our head in the game.

In the next chapter, we will review the principles of ACT and look at how to apply it to other areas such as dealing with pain, and in interactions in teams.

Chapter 8

MANAGING PASSENGERS EVERYWHERE: WRAPPING IT UP AND INTEGRATING YOUR SKILLS

If you worked through this book chronologically, then you should now have a good idea about what you value in your sport. You should also have some clues about the general direction you are heading in, and the next steps you need to take to help improve your performance. You will have met some of your 'monsters' or 'passengers' and got to know them better. They might have become much more familiar, almost like old and annoying buddies that you've been driving around with for half your life or longer. You might even miss them if they were suddenly gone.

We have also looked at skills that allow you to manage your passengers much better should they become too bossy. For example, maybe you discovered that very often some of your passengers were taking turns driving your bus, and that you very seldom sat at the steering wheel. It might have been hard work to get them to sit back in their seats again, and drive the bus yourself; hopefully, the skills we've given you will help you achieve this.

In the previous three chapters, we presented a variety of skills in relation to passengers who were either anxious, lazy, or taking it too easy. Other skills helped with those who were full of self-doubt and who lacked confidence. You might have figured out, for yourself, that some of the skills we discussed specifically for one passenger can easily be used for managing another passenger. This is great. You need to be creative and adaptive, because your passengers are just as creative, and try to outwit you with new tricks!

There are a lot of other passengers in some people's buses that might not seem to fit into any of the categories we discussed so far. Maybe your loudest person on the bus is aching and complaining about being tired or in pain all day long. Or it suggests that you pull back from giving everything to your team because your coach sucks and you want to show them clearly that you are not on board with her suggestions.

The good news is that if you understand the core principles behind the skills you have learned so far, you can easily adapt them to all of these passengers. Let's look at these core principles, and then a few examples.

How to manage bus passengers: Core Skills in a Nutshell

BEING PRESENT AND AWARE

Staying with the bus metaphor, the first skill you need to bring to driving this bus is to be aware of what is going on. This extends to both the many stimuli that are occurring outside your body, and inside your body: mind, body, and environment. If you are not aware of all the different forces pulling on you, then you will very quickly find someone else sitting at the steering wheel, or you'll be unconsciously driving in the wrong direction. Looking at ways to increase your awareness has been a theme of this book. For a review, you can look back over some of the exercises contained in chapters 2, 3, 4, and 5, or look at the list of exercises in the Appendix and pick some you would like to revisit.

Knowing your why, and Doing what matters

In Chapter 3, we looked at Values. This is the WHY that drives you. From working with your Values, you should know what is meaningful to you, and how you want your sporting life to be. You should have a good idea about what you need to do, and some experience in taking action towards your values. If not, it is a good idea to revisit the chapter on Values.

Being open and accepting

There will be times when this is not easy. The temptation to avoid the difficult feelings that some passengers bring up is often present. The skills you have developed to deal with these problems are discussed in the context of the anxious, lacklustre, and low self-worth passengers in Chapters 5 to 7.

In the previous chapters, you learned a number of skills to foster acceptance. Some of these skills are designed to defuse from language and private internal events that are a result of language-based thinking. The following box lists some Defusion techniques for you.

> **Defusion skills**
>
> Below are the defusion exercises you can use and where you can find them in this book. We have included a full list of exercises in Appendix 1 where you can find more, and descriptions of some extra exercises that might be useful.
>
> | | |
> |---|---|
> | The Walk-Through Exercise | Chapter 8 |
> | Leaves on the Stream | Chapter 5 |
> | Mindfulness | Chapter 3 |
> | Carry your thoughts around | Appendix 1 |
> | Milk, Milk, Milk | Appendix 1 |

Being present and aware, knowing the direction you want to move in – and why – and accepting what life presents to you on the way, are the key ingredients for a journey that is in sync with your values. Your journey, rather than your passengers' journey. These ingredients, and the skills you require to express them fully, are similar for most situations you will encounter. So, let's check out what this might look like with a few scenarios and passengers we haven't discussed specifically so far.

Aches and Pains

A lot has been written about pain and dealing with pain (e.g., books on general pain management and on ACT and pain in particular). Hence, we won't go into too much detail. The interested reader might look at books such as 'Acceptance and Commitment Therapy for Chronic Pain' (Dahl, Wilson, Luciano & Hayes, 2005). In this chapter, we simply summarise the essence of an ACT approach in relation to dealing with aches and pains.

When it comes to 'pain', we need to distinguish 'good' and 'bad' pain. 'Good' relates to the sense that acute pain can draw our attention to an injury that we need to deal with, and the pain is often so intense that we cannot continue with certain activities, which means we are also less likely to do more harm to our bodies.

Relating good pain to our bus metaphor – the pain is not an annoying passenger, but a passenger who you want to sit in the driver seat – at that moment – so that it can steer your bus towards protecting your body and maintaining good health in the long term.

Chronic pain is a different issue altogether. In chronic pain, there is a very loose relationship between injured tissue and pain sensation; often, the sending and receiving of pain signals has become the problem, and not the original underlying injury. Here, giving in to the pain passenger, or wasting time and energy struggling with it, has become the issue to deal with. In fact, engaging in experiential avoidance has been shown to be the most powerful predictor for people who develop chronic pain (Dahl, Wilson, Luciano & Hayes, 2005). This book is not the place to discuss the ins and outs of pain signals and the issue of chronic pain in much detail.

While traditional psychological treatments have largely focused on reducing pain or otherwise minimising pain sensations (e.g., through the use of relaxation techniques and distraction), an ACT approach would focus on ending an athlete's struggle with pain, rather than trying to control the pain as such. Remember the Chinese Handcuffs metaphor? Pain is a good example of how any attempt to try to control a negatively evaluated experience might increase suffering. There is plenty of evidence that seems to support the notion that traditional approaches to chronic pain have little lasting effect (van Tulder, Goossens, Waddell, & Nachemson, 2000).

For the purpose of this text, just imagine you have spoken to your physiotherapist or doctor, and you know that the back pain or headache you have often been battling with, is not something that should slow you down; or that you must read it as a signal to take it easy. Once you are clear about that, these signals are part and parcel of the annoying pain passenger trying to take over what you do, and the principles discussed previously apply: being aware, knowing where you are heading, and accepting what is presenting itself to you at any moment.

Another type of 'pain' in sport is the pain and ache that comes from pushing ourselves really hard in training and competition. Pain from our muscles burning when biking up a mountain close to maximum capacity, our lungs aching, our whole body screaming. Here, again, if you are into activities that are extremely demanding, then surely talk to the medical professionals who can guide you in regard to how far you should take it.

Then, when you know you can go all the way to your maximum ability, this aching becomes a distracting passenger too; one that calls out to you, 'Hey, that's enough now', 'Just let up now and you'll be fine, you've done enough already'. Here, we have a passenger whose demands are not in line with your chosen values, and who's there in the back of your bus, but who should not be steering it.

1. Open and aware

Reflect where – in your sporting life – any of the pain passengers mentioned might pop up. Are you prone to take shortcuts in the gym because it's too exhausting, difficult, or painful? Do you start slowing down early in a race because the physical discomfort just seems too unbearable? Make a list of all the places and situations when you are vulnerable. With increased awareness, it will be easier for you to catch your passengers out early when they want to get you off track.

2. Doing what matters

This requires being aware of your purpose. Know exactly WHY you want to climb up that hill at 90 % of your maximum pulse rate. Know why you want to do five sets of lifting weights. This WHY is the answer to your passengers; it's what you keep driving towards when they want to steer you off course, or take shortcuts of any sort.

3. Open and accepting

Our passengers are prone to kick up a fuss. This can be especially troubling when you push yourself. In those situations, you can apply the skills you learned. These skills are there to help you just notice, and not get caught up in the background noise.

You might apply a defusion skill like 'concretising'. You can practise this skill as a full visualisation exercise away from the training session, and then meet your pain in a similar manner when the situation calls for it.

> **Concretising and letting go**
>
> This exercise is similar to the Tin-Can Monster exercise by Hayes & Smith (2005) and is a way of stopping the struggle with your emotions and bodily sensations that are part of the challenges you are face as an athlete.
>
> If you do this exercise by yourself, you might record a script, similar to the one that follows, into your phone and play it back later, leaving enough gaps to allow time to follow each step.
>
> First, choose a challenging situation. This could be a high-pressure situation in a competition, or an everyday sense of dread with certain training routines you have to perform.
>
> Now close your eyes, get comfortable, and take a few deep breaths.

Next, get in touch with the challenging situation you have chosen. Take your time and recall it in your mind as best you can. It will probably help if you remember a recent event where this challenge occurred for you.

Now bring your attention to any bodily sensations or feelings you might experience when you remember this challenge.

Choose one part in your body where you feel it the most. Notice where in your body it begins and ends. What shape does it have? If it had a certain texture, what does it feel like? Is it rather hard, or soft? What temperature does it have? What colour?

Make a mental image of this bodily sensation in this part of your body.

And then drop any resistance to having it there. See if you can simply accept and notice it there. Adopt the stance of a stock-taker who has no personal attachment to the items in a large warehouse, but just notices them there and ticks them off his list.

Then look around and see what else is happening in your body. Focus on one other area in your body where the bodily sensations, in response to recalling this challenge, are quite strong.

Repeat the same process you did before; become aware of the size, shape, and outline of the sensations – maybe even a smell if there is one. Notice any texture that is relevant. If possible, make a mental image of what this looks like.

And, again, let go of any struggle against having these sensations or unwanted thoughts. Just allow them to be there.

Finally, have a quick look around and notice other parts of your body that also have a response to this challenge. These might be things like tension in your neck, butterflies in your stomach, a slight pressure in your head. Just mentally take note of them all; like the stock taker who could not care more or less what is there, but takes notice of it all. Let go of any struggle; accept what is there.

> Take a few more deep breaths and mentally pull the curtain on this exercise; start noticing the world around it and open your eyes.

Dealing with other people

So how do the principles we discussed earlier apply when we operate as a team?

They apply both on the level of the why, and on how, we deal with the specific challenges of working with people.

Nearly all sports involve a team. This is obvious in team sports, but even individual pursuits often involve a team, even if we are not aware of it. This could be a coach, training partners, even family members; anyone who can help or hinder our progress in moving towards our goals. All these individuals can have an impact on performance. If your sport involves a formal team such as a group of players, you will probably be aware that a team does not function at its full potential if the individuals who make it up do not work together. The team itself becomes an entity that needs a joint WHY in order to move harmoniously in one direction. This means working with other people, and seeing where our values fit with those around us, and with the rest of the team.

For every team, it is essential to work out what they value, and the principles they orient themselves towards.

Working out your Values as a Team

Working with others can be difficult for a variety of reasons. A team, however, is a unit. To function effectively, it must have a common goal, a plan, willingness on the part of each member to play a specific part in that plan, and a commitment to supporting others. Underlying these processes are team values, whether they have been articulated or not. All teams have implicit values. Sometimes these are fractured with different sub-groups having different inherent, or unrecognised values. These are the underlying themes that motivate and direct their behaviour. One simple example might be a team member who is driven by the belief that their individual performance is vital, and their focus on that detracts from participating as a co-operative team player.

Attempts to instil team values from above – from the coach, or from an organisation like a club – can work, but can also be heavy-handed and counterproductive. The reason for this is that they are not personal. They did not come directly from the team itself. They are someone else's idea of the values you should have, and you are basically instructed to take them on. They can have a tinge of 'aversive control' about them. As a result, they are often ignored, or even ridiculed by team members. Even if they are values you embrace in other parts of your life, the connection tends not to be made a lot of the time. This is because they lack the personal, emotional element of self-identified values.

When developing team values, it is much more effective to have these identified, and articulated by the team members themselves rather than having them imposed on them by a hierarchy. Although our individual values differ, they are often surprisingly similar. Most people want to be part of the group, get on well with others, perform to a high standard, and to be valued for what they do. When team members can see the similarities between their values and those of teammates it helps forge bonds. Not only can they see each other's motivations, but they can develop team values that embrace what is fundamentally important to each member of the group.

When developing team values, we recommend that individual team members become familiar with their own values and work on those as we have described in Chapter 3. It is then useful to find the values that are common among the team members and develop clear value statements that reflect these. This can be done in several ways. One method is to simply ask the group to describe their highest two or three values. Pick the most prominent of these and develop team values around them. It helps to think broadly here. For example, family and friends are important values for many people. But we can think more broadly about family. Family can also refer to those we choose to spend time with, good friends that we can rely on for example. A team also functions as a mini family. Like a family, there are frictions, but you need each other, and often are stuck with each other, so you need to make the best of it.

If family is a value, how can you relate that to your team? If family or friends are an important value, how would that be demonstrated in your behaviour in the team?

These values can be shown in many ways, from picking up a discarded towel on the changing room floor, to giving a few words of encouragement to a teammate, or putting in an extra sprint to help cover someone having trouble on field. By going through the entire team's most shared values and looking at ways they can be translated into action we can help develop a positive shared vision and clarify actions that will support this.

Team Value Exercise

One way to develop team cohesion and values is to have team members describe their values in small groups of two to three people. Below we give an example of how this might work.

1. In groups of three take turns saying what your three or four main values are. Then

take turns saying what you would be doing if you were living these values. Look at the similarities between your values. Which ones do you share? Which would be useful for the team to develop as part of their collective values? What would these team values look like in action?

2. Change groups and go through the process again with new partners.

3. The team then gives feedback to the whole group on the team values they identified – what they were, and how they might look in action.

4. From this list the group discusses which values they want for the team. They develop simple statements to reflect those values.

That statement might look something like this.

- This team is a family. Each of us is important and though we don't always agree we support each other physically and emotionally.

- We strive for excellence in performance – we are doomed to fall short of our expectations at times but it is the striving that is important. (Mistakes are fine, lack of effort isn't.)

- Self-care is important. We take care of our bodies. This allows us to perform at our best and contribute to the team.

Once the team values are clear, there will be other challenges: conflict with other team members about what path to follow, your own large ego (or someone else's), a sense of unfairness in how your coach handled the selection process, and so on.

Let's look at how you can function in a team with the principles you have learned. Applying these again step by step:

1. Open and aware

Again, start by raising your awareness of yourself in a team, or with other significant people in your sport (your coach, your mates, other supporting people).

Where do passengers get in the way of you being your best? Is it the sulky passenger who does not like the coach telling him what he could do better? Is it the 'big ego' passenger who wants you to always look better than others and be the centre of attention? Again, make a list of all the places and situations when you are vulnerable to not making the best of your interactions with other people.

2. DOING WHAT MATTERS

Now, be mindful of your purpose; if this is working in a team, your purpose should be closely aligned to the purpose and values of your team.

Know exactly WHY you are part of a team, and what values you bring to the team so it can work at its best. These are your individual values.

And there are the values that the team has identified as its driving force. It is important to be aware of how your values fit into the broader team values. A more social team might be about 'having fun together playing a good game of water polo'. A more competitive team might stand for 'excellence in performance' and 'supporting each other to be the best we can'. These values can be less or more formal, depending on the context. A social team will probably not have a workshop on team values, yet – if you reflect on it – this team (like any) has a purpose that is more or less explicit. What is that purpose, and what part of it matters to you?

Integrating mental skill practice into your life

When we ask you to practise any of the exercises, we do not want you to limit yourself to just the five minutes you might be able to free up in your busy day... just one exercise in the morning!

Mental skills exercises can be practised everywhere and anytime. Anxiety and pressures are omnipresent in daily life – at your job, in your relationships and friendships, at play. On your weekend out, asking someone to dance with you can result in inner turmoil, similar to what you might experience in competition. Situations like this are a great ground for practising defusion skills, and commitment to your goals and values. Any time you are doing one thing and your mind gets in the way, or goes off in another direction – or your fears play around with you – you can practise the skills you have learned. So, do it; there does not need to be a break from training.

One of the great things about sport is that a competition is a condensed way of experiencing many of the things that go on in life. There is a beginning, a build-up, a main part, an end. There are things you want to achieve, and challenges you experience along the way. In addition, the skills you learn in your sport can transfer to other aspects of your life and vice versa. Win-win!

This is not simply a nice metaphor, and it won't happen by itself. You can help things by challenging yourself away from the playing field. Set aside a few minutes each morning and think of the challenges you could set for yourself during the day. Then make sure you remind yourself of them throughout the day. And then, go do them. One way of 'doing' might be to look the anxiety passenger in the eye, notice what shows up, and act anyway.

There are challenges everywhere.

Summary

This chapter provided a brief review of what we have covered so far, and introduced some ideas for dealing with other people and for the development of team values. The key points are summarised here.

- One of the themes of this book, and the aim of many of the exercises, has been developing skills to increase your awareness. This involves awareness of what is occurring around you, and also what is happening in your body, and in your thinking. Many of the skills you have learned emphasise increasing awareness, without becoming distracted by internal or external events.

- We have suggested dealing with distractibility and other barriers to performance by developing skills enabling you to be fully open to, and aware of, the full range of your experience. This involved exercises and practice in acceptance, cognitive defusion, being fully in touch with the present moment (as opposed to becoming immersed in thoughts about the present), and in developing a less rigid or limiting view of who or what you are.

These broad areas are summarised in Chapter 2 on The Three Pillars.

- The other main theme of this book has been Engagement; being aware of what is important in your life and dealing with the barriers to living more in line with what you most value. This was covered in Chapter 3, but ideally the values identified in that chapter serve as a guide and motivation for your work in the rest of the book, and in your training and competition.

- This chapter provided some guidance in the functioning of teams and the development of team values.

- Working with others and functioning within a team can be difficult. Managing relationships is necessary if a team is to function effectively. Part of managing these relationships is to be aware that while people are all unique, they are more alike than they are different.

- The development of team values is useful in creating a coherent and effective group, rather than a collection of individuals with different goals.

- Team values need to be developed by the team itself, and not imposed from above. This requires the individuals in a team to have a knowledge of their own core values.

- Finally, we also introduced the Concretising exercise, another acceptance and defusion practice that can help you deal with difficult or intimidating situations.

The next chapter addresses some of the common difficulties people encounter when applying the ACT techniques we have suggested.

Chapter 9

TROUBLE SHOOTING

Throughout this book, you have been introduced to the general principles of ACT and how to apply them in order to improve your sporting performance. This has involved learning a series of specific skills that you can apply in response to various problems. The problems could be dealing with issues of anxiety, poor or variable commitment in training and competition, lack of motivation, or just in dealing with the distracting thoughts and emotions that get in the way of achieving your best.

The techniques of this book are aimed at helping you become less distractible, more aware, focused, and committed.

You may have noticed that we repeatedly make certain points across the book, such as the shifting attention to physical reality, and giving less prominence to your thinking mind. We have repeated themes like this and introduced exercises that have a similar purpose, partly because – in essence – ACT is very simple. At least the ideas are straightforward.

- Pay attention (Really pay attention).
- Allow yourself to fully **physically** experience your emotions.
- Don't get wrapped up in your thoughts.
- Shift awareness to what is important to you, and what you are doing.
- Fully commit to the activity you are engaged in.

Or, simply, be Open, Aware, and Engaged.

That seems fairly basic, and describing these steps is easy. But, like most things, doing it – executing the desired skill – is very different from talking about it, or daydreaming about doing it. It takes practice. Lots of practice. If you have diligently worked your way through this book, you will probably have noticed some changes in your awareness and in your behaviour. If so, that is great. However, to keep the skills you have learned, sharp, you will probably need to keep up some practice. This will vary from person to person, depending on their goals, and the things they find difficult.

Values is a concept that is very useful to remind yourself about. We all tend to drift into doing 'what needs to be done' every day, on semi-automatic, without thinking about the bigger picture; such as why the things we are doing are important to us. This means our values can get lost as we are focused on day-to-day tasks. At the very least, this means that we miss out on some positive reinforcement, and key factors that sustain our motivation can be lost. At worst, we can end up devoting most of our time to things that aren't important to us, while we lose sight of those things that make life meaningful. Revisiting the values exercises can be helpful, as is having reminders around you that help you step back and look at the bigger picture. This can be as simple as having motivational reminders like pictures, sayings, or books that you find inspirational; or a list of your valued activities displayed where you are likely to see them, reminding you of what matters most to you.

Mindfulness is another important skill that needs attention. It underlies many of the other skills you have learned. It requires developing your attentional abilities, while increasing acceptance of unwanted feelings, and defusion from the thought machine that wants to blind you with a sort of virtual reality; a selective interpretation of what is happening and of your self-worth.

We hope you have noticed that mindfulness dovetails into, and supports, other exercises we have suggested. It is a skill, though, and one that can degrade if you don't practice it. We are not suggesting that you need to become a long-term serious meditator – practicing for hours a day – but short, regularly scheduled practice sessions of the core mindfulness exercise will be useful in maintaining and building on your abilities to defuse from thoughts, and accept what is happening, while still engaging in actions that aren't always easy. Like dealing with angry family members, or going to train when it is cold, wet, and miserable outside. Mindfulness seems to help foster goal-directed behaviour, or to phrase it another way, reduces distraction and procrastination.

If you have a problem that keeps recurring – like fear of failure, performance anxiety, or inappropriate anger – it is important to keep doing the suggested exercises. Particularly the use of the

Diary of Reactive Habits, along with the Walk-Through, and Lean In exercises. They will help you get used to unwanted thoughts and emotions without getting lost in them and acting out on them. You will become defused or separate from them, in a way, and it is easier to have them not impact on your behaviour.

If you have had difficulty with a particular exercise in the book, go back and try it a few times. Often, it will eventually 'click'. You can also look at the Appendix and find alternate exercises that target the same function. For everyone, it can be useful to go back and re-read chapters, and to go through the exercises again. Sometimes, things are different on repetition, and new insights, or areas of avoidance become apparent.

The way to look at the development of these ACT skills is not as something 'extra' we do once to get a result, but as part of our development. It is a journey that doesn't end. We can keep using the same skills, exercises, and practices to improve our performance as circumstances continue to change and we meet new obstacles. Or, as often happens, the old challenges come back slightly disguised and try to divert us off course.

Below, we have highlighted some common problems that come up in practising these skills and have offered some suggestions for how to deal with them. It is useful to read all of these summaries, but feel free to skip to those that are not most relevant to you in the first instance.

I don't want to accept feeling bad!

Yep. We know. And, if things are working fine for you, then you may not need to accept things you don't like. Maybe ignoring things or avoiding them is working fine. If you can change things for the better and not accept them, great. As long as that works for you. When we suggest accepting, we are talking about those things we can't change. This can be unwanted thoughts that just come up or keep repeating, or emotions and physical sensations that we don't want, and that end up driving our behaviour. When we get fused with thoughts, or our actions are driven by avoidance – and this impacts negatively on our performance – we need to look at ways of dealing with these habits. If the control strategy – avoid, suppress, and change – hasn't worked by now, then developing acceptance skills along with some committed action might be the only viable option.

And it is not easy. Nobody wants to feel bad, and we all know the pull to avoid uncomfortable feelings. To actively engage with the unwanted feelings, even fairly minor ones, takes courage, commitment, and knowledge of how to go about it (without wallowing in it), and ideally with some support.

Basically, if it was easy, we wouldn't need to write a book about it. We suggest you just keep plugging away at it. Really, what alternative do you have?

I don't get mindfulness

For many people, it doesn't matter how mindfulness works, they are willing to try it, and if it is of value for them – if it is useful – then they practise. For others, it is important to know how things work. They need a deeper understanding before they fully commit to things. They want to understand the nuts and bolts of it. Why should I do this? How does it work? What is the evidence that it can help? It is important that this information is available; however, that would take a book of its own. So, here we will provide a very brief summary.

For our purposes, how does mindfulness work? Most of our thinking, as adults, is based on thoughts. A primarily cognitive, symbolic, verbally-based way of thinking. But this is not our only way of experiencing things. In fact, before about 16 months of age, we didn't have a well-developed verbal ability; our language is limited, so our experiences are quite different. Once language really kicks in, at around 16-months of age, we start to make judgments and inferences, develop fears, expectations, have imaginary futures, and feared pasts. What is really interesting is that the thoughts we have are not simply logical ideas; they have a very real, and strong, somatic component. We feel them in our bodies. In other words, you can't have a thought without a feeling going along with it (technically, this is called the transformation of stimulus functions). Often, these feelings or associations are quite familiar, and mild, and go unnoticed as they are so common and unconcerning... but some are very strong. If you think about it, you will have quite common but variable reactions to lots of things. You might think about eating something, liver for instance, and think it is horrible. This is associated with a slight, or perhaps strong physical reaction to thinking about it, while other people will like it and feel positive, and others will be neutral. Your favourite flavour of ice cream will create a different set of reactions. The key is that it is not the thoughts that drive our behaviour, but the feelings that are associated with them.

What mindfulness does is bring us back to what is current. To actual physical reality. Mindfulness practice doesn't stop thinking, but it helps us to not go down the familiar, well-worn tracks of assumptions, and associated feelings that we have built up over time. It is basically practice in allowing those feelings and thoughts without supporting them (without keeping them going), so they fade on their own. As a result, we can experience situations (eating ice cream, or liver) as they are right now; rather than how our old habits of reacting tell us.

Mindfulness is exposure therapy and reality therapy wrapped up together. It allows us to step out of the virtual world we have created for ourselves into reality. We step out of our habitual patterns of thinking, expectations, and associations to see what is actually going on. It is like stepping out of the Matrix. Not easy, but liberating.

For those interested in the scientific background to this topic we suggest that, in the first instance, you look at the literature on Relational Frame Theory. The book, Relational Frame Theory (2013) by Steve Hayes, Dermot Barnes-Holmes, and Bryan Roche is a good place to start. This provides a general background on how thinking works. An easy to understand version is included in Steve Hayes' book, Get Out of Your Mind and Into Your Life. There is also the work of Paul Ekman on the duration of emotions. Paul has some talks on YouTube that may be helpful, and has written books for the general public. You could also look at the various studies on the effects of mindfulness meditation on attention, emotion, and mood states like depression and anxiety. This research paints a compelling picture regarding the usefulness of mindfulness.

I can't do mindfulness

This is something quite a few people feel. It is typically based on either a slight misunderstanding of what mindfulness is, or a need to learn how to simply allow the attention to rest on something simple like the physical sensations of breathing.

For some people, they feel their mind is racing too much when they practice mindfulness. This is fine. Just allow it, and as much as possible include awareness of bodily sensations in your practice. Just don't allow yourself to get caught up in the thoughts, and gently return to awareness of the body. For others, they feel they are not aware of anything at all. It is important to remember that everyone has the necessary skills to practice mindfulness. If you can breathe and attend to things... you can do it. In fact, you have probably often been 'mindful' in the past without being aware of it. The key is to practise letting go of expectations while allowing the physical experience of breathing. It is a sort of active non-doing, which some people who are quite anxious can feel uncomfortable with. It is worth persevering. If you find it really difficult, then learning a relaxation technique like Progressive Muscle Relaxation is useful.

This helps you focus on bodily sensations, builds attentional capacity, and helps relaxation. After developing some experience with this, engage with mindfulness of the breath.

Remember, it is mindfulness practice. It is not perfect, unwavering, complete mindfulness. It is practice, and as in all practice we learn from our mistakes. As the great Zen Master, Wumen, said in his cautions on Zen practice, 'To be alert and never unclear is to wear chains and an iron yoke'.

Don't wear chains and an iron yoke. Just sincerely do your best.

I don't have time

Yes, you do.

If you had time to read this far... you have time. Make time. Carve out 15 minutes a day, several days a week, if you have to. Drop some non-essential activity – phone surfing, or daydreaming. Run through some of the exercises while getting a drink. Force yourself to get up 15 minutes early and do some practice.

Remember, you can have little mini-mindfulness practice sessions while doing the things you normally do, walking, standing in line, tying your shoes. I believe it was Aesop who said, 'Slow and steady wins the race'.

When I do mindfulness, I don't have anythoughts

That is ok. The aim of mindfulness is not to notice your thoughts.

If you don't notice yourself having thoughts while practicing mindfulness, you are either: in a deep state of absorption with no thoughts occurring, you just didn't notice them because you are very distractible, or you can't remember because you zoned out in a daydream. In any of those instances, the solution is the same. Try to develop a clear awareness of the bodily sensations that come up as the breath moves in and out. If you find it hard to notice any sensations in your body, keep with it – maintaining an open, almost expectant, slightly curious awareness regarding the body. If you still have difficulty connecting with the body, practice Progressive Muscle Relaxation for a week or so, and continue your mindfulness of breath practice after this.

I can't do the values exercise

Some people have trouble with identifying Values. One way to overcome this is to think, would I do this if nobody knew about it? Would I do it for pure joy, or because it is important to me? Another way to identify Values is to check out how you feel during and after different activities. Do you feel satisfied, or happy, or content? If so, that activity is probably supporting a larger Value. Often, we only really become aware of what is important in our lives when major things happen – weddings, births, deaths, losing jobs, or friends. But valued activities are probably all around you. Washing the dishes would not fit the criteria for a Value, but it could be satisfying as it contributes to self-care or being a good partner or flatmate. Look for the Value behind your usual activities.

Visualisation exercises like the ones we suggested in the chapter on Values can be difficult for some people. If that is the case, try some of the exercises suggested previously to identify your Values.

All my values are high

This is generally due to a lack of clarity around what is really important to you. One way to tackle this is to seriously and systematically go through your Values and force yourself to rate them in priority. List some activities that support these Values, and as suggested earlier, notice how you feel when you do them. Which are most satisfying? Which are most meaningful? Which would you not want to give up forever? Another thing you can do is to imagine you only had 24 hours to engage in valued activity, that's it. No second chances. What would you choose to do?

I made changes but after a week or so I fall back into the s ame old habits

As the old song says, 'Everybody wants to go to heaven, but nobody wants to die'. Or, for our purposes, we all want things to be different, but we don't want to change what we do.

We all drift back into old habits because what we know is comfortable and, well, a habit. In many ways, the commitment part of Acceptance and Commitment Therapy is the hardest. That is because to make changes you need to just keep going back and doing it again, and again, and again. This seems to be part of the human condition. Change takes effort.

Another way of thinking about it is like learning to ride a bike. If you learn to ride a bike as a child, you fall off a lot. You probably hurt yourself as well. Once you have learned, though, you never forget it. You can just do it. It is automatic. That is what the skills taught in this book are like. Do them enough, and you will have them; and, you will be able to use them again and again and again.

Conclusion

We hope you have found this book helpful and will continue to refer to – and use – the exercises suggested, exploring them in greater detail over time. A list of exercises used in this book, where to find them, and what ACT functions they target are included in Appendix 1. We have also included some additional exercises you might like to try in this Appendix.

Meeting our goals, and even managing to consistently follow a plan of action, or a training schedule designed to meet these goals, is rarely easy. A clear focus of using ACT in performance enhancement is on Values; that is, on what is important to you. Awareness of, and calling to mind from time to time, what drives you, what you want, and what you find fulfilling will greatly aid motivation. It is essentially a focus on chasing the good (appetitive control) as opposed to running away from feared failures. But, as we know, this is rarely easy. Commitment, the 'C' part of ACT, is simply getting up again and again after each failure and setback. That is what breeds success, however you might define it. It is this process that defines our lives. Not what we achieve but how we act. What we do.

Good Luck.
Jim and Christoph

Appendix 1

A List of ACT Exercises

Below is a list of different ACT exercises, and where you can find them in this book. Some of them you will have practised as you worked through the book. Others are described, below, in order to give you alternatives that you might find work better for you or your team. We have organised them by the ACT function or process they are most closely associated with: Openness, Awareness, or Engagement. Of course, many of these exercises help develop more than one ACT-related skill. If you think about it, a little, engaging in any of these exercises is related to Engagement. That is to take Committed Action to live more closely in line with your Values.

ACT Exercises by Function

DEFUSION

Exercise	Specific ACT Skills	Where	Pillar
Leaves on the Stream	Defusion Self-As-Context	Chapter 5	Openness
Thought/Feeling record	Defusion Acceptance Self-As-Context	Chapter 2	Openness
The Finger Exercise	Defusion	Chapter 2	Openness
Diary of Reactive Habits	Defusion Acceptance	Chapter 4	Openness Awareness
Mindfulness	Defusion Acceptance	Chapter 2	Openness Awareness
Monsters on the Bus – Exercise 1 & 2	Defusion Acceptance	Chapter 4	Openness Awareness

Exercise	Specific ACT Skills	Where	Pillar
The Walk-Through Exercise	Defusion Acceptance	Chapter 7	Openness
Concretising and letting go	Defusion Acceptance	Chapter 8	Openness
Milk, Milk, Milk	Defusion	Described Below	Openness
I am having…	Defusion Self-As-Context	Described Below	Openness Awareness
Carrying negative thoughts around	Defusion Acceptance Self-As-Context	Described Below	Openness Awareness

ACCEPTANCE

Exercise	Specific ACT Skill	Where	Pillar
Mindfulness	Acceptance Defusion	Chapter 2	Openness Awareness

Exercise	Specific ACT Skill	Where	Pillar
Diary of Reactive Habits	Acceptance Defusion	Chapter 4	Openness Awareness
Monsters on the Bus – Exercise 3	Acceptance Defusion	Chapter 4	Openness Awareness
Leaning in Exercise	Acceptance	Chapter 5	Openness
Chinese Handcuffs	Acceptance	Chapter 5	Openness
Holding the Breath Exercise	Acceptance	Chapter 6	Openness
The Walk-Through Exercise	Acceptance Defusion	Chapter 7	Openness

VALUES

Exercise	Specific ACT Skill	Where	Pillar
Funeral Exercise	Identify Values	Chapter 3	Engagement
Tombstone Exercise	Identify Values	Chapter 3	Engagement
Values Questionnaire	Identify Values	Chapter 3	Engagement
80th Birthday Exercise	Identify Values	Chapter 3	Engagement
Bull's Eye Exercise	Identify Values	Chapter 3	Engagement
Monsters on the Bus – Exercise 4	Committed Action	Chapter 4	Engagement
Independence Exercise	Committed Action	Chapter 6	Engagement
Acting As If	Committed Action	Chapter 6	Engagement
Two Sides of the Coin	Committed Action	Chapter 6	Engagement

Exercise	Specific ACT Skill	Where	Pillar
Team Values	Identify Values & Committed Action	Chapter 8	Engagement

Additional Exercises

CARRY YOUR THOUGHTS AROUND

Another way to help defuse from intrusive, or unhelpful, thoughts is to carry them around with you. Write down the thoughts you tend to be fused with. For most people, these are negative thoughts about themselves, or their abilities. It is good to have small cards, like blank business cards (you can get these at stationary, or office supply stores) or just write them down on a piece of paper. Put them in your pocket, purse, or wallet and carry them with you. If they are in a purse, wallet, or computer bag, make sure they are not somewhere you will not be aware of them. The idea is to be reminded that they are there.

It is a good idea to take them out and read them at least twice a day. This helps you emotionally connect with the thoughts, and reminds you they are there. When reading them, take your time and read through them slowly. Feel whatever comes up as you fully allow the thoughts. Over time, these practices aid defusion, and you see thoughts just as thoughts. Nothing more.

Robyn Walser, a Psychologist and well-known ACT trainer, suggests that people in her groups write their negative thoughts on sticky notes (post-it notes), or on a card, and then tape it to them. Sometimes this means that a person is covered in negative thoughts. Then everybody goes and takes their thoughts with them while they chat together during a tea break. You might want to try this one at home. Tape as many negative thoughts about yourself or your abilities that you can think of onto your upper body and – if necessary – your legs... then go about your normal business for a couple of hours. With this exercise, you are very literally carrying your thoughts around. See what happens when you do. Does it feel different writing them down compared to thinking about them? How does it feel taping them to yourself? Does it feel different after half an hour or so? What does it feel like if someone knocks at the door, or a family member or flatmate comes home? This is a great exercise that really aids defusion.

This can be a very challenging exercise which, when done in groups, brings up very powerful emotions. Therefore, we suggest that only very experienced ACT therapists use this exercise in a group training situation. Another, less threatening, version of this exercise is to imagine you have a negative thought about yourself printed in big, bold letters on a t-shirt you are wearing as you walk down the street.

'Milk, Milk, Milk...'

This is perhaps the classic defusion exercise. It is based on the fact that words carry emotional/somatic meaning, and that they lose their power on repetition. In the original, or training version of this exercise, you simply say the word 'milk'. Say it slowly a few times and notice what you feel. For people who drink milk regularly, they will generally begin to feel a milky type of taste in their mouth. You could also use something like 'ice cream' or 'cheeseburger' if that works better for you. Then repeat the word, out loud, for between three to five minutes. At first, say it slowly while trying to connect with any sensations or images that come up. Then, after a minute or so, say it faster. Just keep repeating it. Try not to smile or think of other things (avoidance strategies) and keep saying it. What happens?

For nearly everyone, the word begins to become meaningless gibberish. It has no meaning. Some people have said it eventually sounds like birds in the background, or a running stream.

Now, for your defusion exercise, pick a word or a short phrase that you are fused with. One you want to avoid, and not pay attention to. 'I am useless' or 'I am a loser' are phrases many people find difficult. But it is important that you pick a word that is relevant to you, and one that brings up some unwanted emotions. You can also shorten the phrase once you have emotionally connected with the unwanted feeling saying something like 'loser', or 'useless'. You can also use longer phrases if that fits your situation. 'If I miss this shot, they will laugh at me' might be one example. It is, however, useful to shorten the phrases over time to keep the emotional connection as long as possible. 'They will laugh at me' or 'laugh at me' would work once you had the situation clearly in mind.

Then simply repeat that word out loud just as you did for 'milk'. Repeat it again and again and again – while trying to be aware of any physical sensations/emotions that come up. Try to feel them while repeating the word. Time this and make it at least three full minutes, five minutes is better.

- Start to say it faster for a while,
- Then slow it down again,
- Say it faster and faster and faster
- Keep with it
- Then, after a while, say it in a very deep, booming voice for 15 or 20 seconds
- Then say it in a high squeaky voice
- If you can do a funny voice, or an accent, use that

What happened to the meaning of the word over time?

Were the feelings as strong as you went on?

Were they as negative as when you first said the word out loud?

This is an excellent exercise for defusing from unwanted thoughts or assumptions about ourselves. When doing it, you are effectively feeling the negative feelings, and hearing the words over and over. And, they lose their power.

'Acceptance'

Small acceptance exercises can be practised literally anywhere, anytime. These can also be considered mini-mindfulness exercises, or as simply allowing things to be as they are. This type of exercise helps build the habits of awareness, attending to physical reality, and allowing – or accepting – thoughts and physical sensations. This is an alternative to being avoidant, or wanting to get rid of our feelings, or to being lost in our thoughts.

Some examples might be:

- Walking out into the cold, and instead of hunching over and guarding against the elements, simply feel the cold air, the rush of it down your collar, and – if it is raining – simply feel it against your skin, and your clothes. In a similar way, you can attend to the air, the temperature, and the wind on your skin any time you step outside; briefly being aware of where you are and what you feel.

- Feeling what is under, or in your hands. Your hands on the steering wheel of a car when at the traffic lights, a bag you are carrying, the feel and weight of a plate or a cup.

- The weight of your body in bed. The feel of the blankets or duvet. A sense of warmth or cold.

- Attending to the sensations in the entire body when stretching.

- When you are frustrated, such as held up on the way home or when going to work, be aware of the feelings in your body. What sensations go along with the feeling of being frustrated? What does your face feel like? Don't try to change anything. Just be aware and allow the feelings, without acting on them.

References

Aitken, R., (trans.), (1991). The Gateless Barrier (The Wu-men Kuan). New York, NY: North Point Press.

Cayoun, B. A., Francis, S. E., & Shires, A. G. (2019). The clinical handbook of Mindfulness-integrated Cognitive Behavior Therapy: A step-by-step guide for therapists. Hoboken, NJ: Wiley.

Csikszentmihalyi, M., (1990). Flow: The psychology of optimal experience. New York: Harper & Row.

Dahl, J. C., & Lundgren, T. L. (2006). Living beyond your pain: Using Acceptance and Commitment Therapy to ease chronic pain. Oakland, CA: New Harbinger.

Dahl, J.C., Wilson, K.G., Luciano, C., & Hayes S.C. (2005). Acceptance and Commitment Therapy for Chronic Pain. Oakland: Harbinger.

Davidson, R. J., & Lutz, A. (2008). Buddha's Brain: Neuroplasticity and Meditation. IEEE signal processing magazine, 25(1), 176–174. https://doi.org/10.1109/msp.2008.4431873

Edwards, T., Kieran, K., Hardy, L., & Gould, D. (2002). A Qualitative Analysis of Catastrophic Performances and the Associated Thoughts, Feelings, and Emotions. The Sport Psychologist. 16, 1-19

Eifert, G.H., & Forsyth J.P. (2005). Acceptance & Commitment Therapy for Anxiety Disorders. Oakland: New Harbinger.

Eifert, G.H. & Heffner, M. (2003). The effects of acceptance versus control contexts on avoidance of panic-related symptoms. Journal of Behavior Therapy and Experimental Psychiatry, 34, 293-312

Gallwey, W. T. (1997). The Inner Game of Tennis. The classic guide to the mental side of peak performance. New York: Random House.

Gardner, F.L., & Moore, Z.E. (2007). The psychology of enhancing human performance: The Mindfulness-Acceptance-Commitment (MAC) approach. New York: Spring Publishing.

Hayes, S. C., Barnes-Holmes, D., & Roche, B. (Eds.). (2001). Relational frame theory: A post-Skinnerian account of human language and cognition. Kluwer Academic/Plenum Publishers.

Hayes, S.C. & Smith, S. (2005). Get out of your mind and into your life: the new acceptance and commitment therapy. Oakland: New Harbinger.

Hayes, S. C., Strohsal, K. D., Wilson, K. G. (1999). Acceptance and Commitment Therapy: An experiential approach to behaviour change. New York: Guilford Press.

Jones, G., Hanton, S., & Swain, A.B.J. (1994). Intensity and interpretation of anxiety symptoms in elite and nonelite sports performers. Personality and Individual Differences, 17, 657-663.

Kayes, D. C., (2006). Destructive goal pursuit: The Mt. Everest Disaster. New York: Palgrave Macmillan.

Langer, E., (2009). Counterclockwise: mindful health and the power of possibility. New York: Ballantine.

Lundgren, T., Louma, J., Dahl, J., Strohsal, K., & Melin, L (2012) The Bull's-Eye values survey: a psychometric evaluation, Cognitive and Behavior Practice, (19), 518-526

Naito, E., & Hirose, S. (2014). Efficient foot motor control by Neymar's brain. Frontiers in human neuroscience, 8, 594. https://doi.org/10.3389/fnhum.2014.00594

Schneider, M. (2014, July 17). Das 7:1 gegen Brasilien war beklemmend. Der Stern

Strosahl, K., Robinson, P., & Gustavsson, T. (2012). Brief Interventions for radical change: principles & practice of focused acceptance & commitment therapy. Oakland, CA: New Harbinger Publications.

van Tulder M., Goossens, M., & Waddell, G, (2000). Conservative treatment of chronic low back pain. In Nachemson, A., & Jonsson. E., (Eds.) Neck and back pain: The scientific evidence of causes, diagnosis, and treatment. Philadelphia, PA: Lippincott, Williams & Wilkins.

www.ingramcontent.com/pod-product-compliance
Lightning Source LLC
Chambersburg PA
CBHW080410170426
43194CB00015B/2769